HOW OUR BRAINS BETRAY US

CHANGE THE WAY YOU THINK AND MAKE
BETTER DECISIONS BY UNDERSTANDING THE
COGNITIVE BIASES AND HEURISTICS THAT
DESTROY OUR LIVES!

MAGNUS MCDANIELS

Special Bonus

Want this book for free?

Get free unlimited access to it and all of my
new books by joining my fanbase!

Scan With
Your
Camera to
Join!

CONTENTS

Introduction   5

1. Survivorship Bias   11
2. Confirmation Bias   21
3. Availability Heuristic   29
4. Loss Aversion Bias (Prospect Theory)   37
5. Hindsight Bias   45
6. Anchoring Bias (Priming)   51
7. Egocentric Bias   65
8. Pygmalion Effect Bias   73
9. Halo Effect Bias   79
10. Decision Fatigue Bias   85
11. Sunk Cost Fallacy   91
12. Reciprocation Tendency   97
13. Dunning Kruger Effect   105
14. The Ben Franklin Effect   115
15. Cognitive Dissonance   123
16. Decoy Effect   129
17. The Spotlight Effect   137
18. The Ikea Effect   143
19. Fundamental Attribution Error (False   149
    Attribution Bias)
20. Bandwagon Effect   155
21. Framing Effect   161
22. Extension Neglect   167
23. Zero Risk   173
24. Ostrich Effect   179
25. Naive Realism   187
26. Self-Serving Bias   193
27. Baader-Meinhof Phenomenon   199

28. Plan Continuation Bias   205
29. The Gambler's Fallacy   211
30. Curse of Knowledge Bias   217
31. The Law of Small Numbers   225
32. Social Proof   233
33. Fear of Missing Out (FOMO)   245
34. The Lollapalooza Tendency   253

Conclusion   259
References   267

INTRODUCTION

The human brain is powerful. It controls our thoughts, our thoughts then control our actions, and our actions influence the results we each see in our day-to-day lives. However, this power is not without consequences.

Your brain is not designed for success; it's designed for survival. Because of hundreds of thousands of years of evolution, our brains developed shortcuts and limitations to further help us survive. These shortcuts, referred to as cognitive biases, were very efficient. They helped us spend less time in deep thought and more time focused on what really mattered—survival. We often needed to take imme-diate actions that would most benefit our needs, like reacting fast to a fight-or-flight situation, getting food, accessing water and shelter, and reproducing. Thus, our brains became self-optimized to focus on these basic needs.

This worked great for the time.These biases made sure we focused on what really mattered and gave us shortcuts in our thinking to save time and become more efficient. However, we do NOT live in that world today. These cognitive biases that were developed to help us survive in a world we lived in as cave dwellers are not always helpful to us in the modern world. They can really f#$k us over in today's digital age if we aren't aware of them.

These biases are more powerful than is widely understood. It's unfortunate that so many people go about their lives totally unaware that these subconscious biases drive many of their actions on a daily basis. So many prejudices people exhibit toward the "other " make life in a multicultural society like the United States more stressful than it has to be. As you will learn in this book, the biases that caused people to make snap judgements for their own survival often do not work these days, when understanding becomes a key to keeping the peace among a restive populace.

You've probably seen examples of these cognitive biases in your life. Have a friend who dropped out of college to start their big business idea? How did that turn out? Let me guess: it failed (like the other 98 percent of businesses that fail in the first year) and they ended up going back to school to finish their degree ten years later. They have fallen prey to survivorship bias, and I cover that in Chapter 1 (Survivorship Bias).

How about the friend who is constantly on social media and judging others based on their social profiles? Let me guess, they also think reality TV is very accurate and resembles what their real-life expectations should be. Anyone who does some digging can see that these big social media influencers are often NOT what they present themselves to be in real life. Real life is NOT going to end up like something you saw on a reality TV show, and expecting it to be that way is just setting yourself up for disaster. Also, people often cannot conceive of a reality that differs from their own, and for that, they are worse off. This is naïve realism, and I discuss it in Chapter 25.

I've seen all the previous examples in my own life, with personal friends of mine. Hell, I've fallen victim to several biases myself, only to realize much later just how big of a mistake I made. One time during a salary negotiation, a hiring manager kept anchoring my salary down to his baseline. Early in the conversation, he threw out some lowball number and then hardly budged. This led me to settling for a much lower salary than I had anticipated. I realize now that this is a common negotiation tactic that interviewers use early in the conversation. That's why I started keeping notes and learning about every fundamental bias that has the potential to screw me over. After some time, my notes became so cumbersome that I decided to just put everything together into a clear and concise book, hoping it would help others avoid these same mistakes. I've provided some short memorable stories with each example really to drill home the cost/benefit of each bias.

One thing has become clear to me over time: the more aware we are of these biases, the more we can avoid them and thus improve our lives. Conversely, we can also use these biases to our advantage in certain situations to ensure we get the best results life offers. For example, if you know about the bandwagon effect in Chapter 20, maybe you can jump off in time. Business people, or really anyone, who knows about the sunk cost fallacy discussed in

Chapter 11 or the plan continuation bias in Chapter 28 will know to stop throwing good money after bad.

Most people fall victim to these biases every day, while only a select few are avoiding them and actually using them to their advantage. Which group do you want to be in? Be careful what you wish for; once you pick up on and master these biases in your day-to-day life, it becomes ever more difficult to not notice them. You'll start seeing them everywhere.

In the chapters that follow, I not only describe these biases and provide some memorable examples of them at work, I also include advice given by experts to help resolve the hold they have over all of us. And in the conclusion I go more in depth on how all of them work and possible ways to counteract them by referring to a book that made a huge impact on me years ago: *Thinking, Fast and Slow* by one of the greats in the study of biases, Daniel Kahneman.

1

SURVIVORSHIP BIAS

Beware of advice from the successful.

— BARNABY JAMES

Survivorship bias is a fairly common error that comes to bear often in business decisions but is fairly common in many endeavors. This bias occurs when those measuring or quantifying what it takes to be successful eliminate failures from the sample. If they had considered the failures as well, their predictions for future success could well have been very different.

Survivorship bias can lead to overly optimistic conclusions because people never consider their failures. The bias could be in favor of the living vs. the dead, the successful vs. the failures, the beautiful or attractive vs. the average or ugly. For example, people sometimes believe the music of the past is so much better than music now. However, they fail to consider that the music from the past that is still being listened to today has stood the test of time; an old-time hit that people still love once had a lot of competitors that bit the dust and faded into oblivion.

Or, people might opine how much more beautiful architecture was in the past compared to what is being built today. They do not consider that build-ings are being razed and something constructed in their place all the time. Only a few buildings, what people consider the best or most beautiful buildings, for various reasons, have been left standing for folks to admire.

The same applies to clothing or furniture now housed in museums. These are the best of the best; almost all of such ancient possessions got thrown out long ago. Likewise, any old machinery seen functioning in the present is not an example of "they don't build 'em like they used to." Those goods and items of lesser quality have been junked or otherwise disposed of.

Career Choices and Underestimating the Chance of Failure

Survivorship bias can wreak havoc on the choices an individual makes in life, starting from a very early age, that can have a long-range impact on their ability to earn a living. Young people who reason, "Hey, Steve Jobs dropped out of college and became an immense success. I can too!" may be in for a serious surprise. For every Steve Jobs, there are thousands who were brilliant and as determined as Jobs, yet who failed. If they do not consider their failures when making this decision, a young person may have forfeited college and a lucrative career for a pipe dream. Truth be told, a majority of the United States' successful business people graduated from college—a whopping 94 percent, to be exact.

Survivorship bias often creates a false perception that a person can achieve great things if they only try hard enough, but that is not necessarily the case. Survivorship bias leads people to ignore the actual cause of an event and its effect. Correlations seem obvious to them when some elements are only due to chance. They want a coherent success story and survivorship bias helps them ignore the failures, because these judgements are taking place on an unconscious level.

Survivorship bias has support from the culture, from everyone else's survivorship bias that spawns books, movies, TV shows, and examples from real life. There is no market for a dreary tale of failure, a sad story of stepping down the social ladder instead of up to new heights of achievement. Also, what is unusual or vivid spurs on the media to report these accounts of fantastical achievement in the face of grinding poverty. The gleaming face of one person who has escaped the slums sells TV shows and profits advertisers; the pitiful story of those who remain behind, caught up in poverty year after year, do not.

Even such a staid market as the one that exists for business books does not escape this bias for the unusual, the glamorous, this story of success against all odds. When they draw upon examples, many business authors lionize misfit billionaires for their risk-taking behavior, when maybe the billionaires succeeded despite their behavior, not because of it. The writers do not consider failures—that someone from a different background who started their business at the wrong time did not succeed when they engaged in risky entrepreneurship, because with every success thousands of would-be actors, musicians, artists, and entrepreneurs fail every day.

Almost every single generic presentation for startups starts with, "Ninety-five percent of all startups fail," but rarely do we pause for a moment and think, "What does this really mean?" We nod our heads in somber acknowledgement and with great enthusiasm turn to the heroes who made it — Zuckerberg, Gates, etc., to absorb pearls of wisdom and find the Holy Grail of building successful companies. Learning from the successful is a much deeper problem and can reduce the probability of success more than we might imagine (Samir Rath and Teodora Georgieva, 2014).

Legends about success are just that—legends. Outsiders writing business books may tell them, but the crazy billionaires hope to add to the mystique. They may all have forgotten the days when they drove a jalopy and worked out of their garage. Or those stories, too, are food for the legend. They may kid themselves with the hindsight bias (Chapter 5) and believe that they planned it all.

When deciding on the best path forward, consider the example of Abraham Wald, whose story I tell at the end of this chapter. Wald succeeded in the mission to armor WWII bombers by considering all the bombers that started on the same path but did not make it.

In Academia, the Survivors are the Advisors

Survivorship bias is rife in academia because those who are there to advise students are the ones who made it through: the survivors. When the tenured faculty assume that all aspiring academics share their own circumstances, the bias can spell ill outcomes for the students who do not share their privileges.

For example, some senior researchers simply assume their graduate assistants can afford to work without pay when such is not the case, especially if they live in an expensive city. After all, they aided researchers without pay, so why should their students not face similar circumstances? If these senior researchers could afford to work without pay back in the day, most likely they come from a privileged background. They also might not have had other demands on their time, such as caring for children.

For these reasons, survivorship bias in career advice becomes self-perpetuating. Those who survived and thrived because of privilege assume that those hoping to follow in their footsteps are in similar financial and social situations; conversely, those who lack that privilege are less likely to make it to a position from which they can give less biased advice (Dave Hemprich-Bennett, Dani Rabaiotti and Emma Kennedy, 2021).

Academic advisors would be well-advised to find out from their students what barriers they might be facing so that they can really help them progress in their chosen field. This might be the key to reducing inequities in academic careers.

The Funds that Did Not Survive

When making an investment in a mutual fund, people risk a smaller return on investment than expected if they only know the returns of successful funds and not those of funds that have failed. This can occur with mutual funds if a company has closed its poorly performing funds and does not include those funds in their data (Investopedia). Therefore, people should not base their investment decisions only on past performance.

Researchers eliminated survivorship bias in the mutual fund industry when they followed returns on all funds existing at the end of 1976. They found many researchers came to mistaken conclusions by failing to include the bias in analyzing fund performance. Elton et al. (1996) measured for the bias as the average for the surviving fund minus the risk-adjusted return over the S&P 500. This figure turned out to be 0.9 percent per year for the entire US mutual fund industry

A company risks legal consequences under state and federal truth in advertising laws if it exploits this bias. For example, they advertise a product to a certain population as a product with a high success rate, but this success rate depends on tests of a different population than the one they targeted. The company faces consequences after being notified about its false advertising practices and yet persists in its behavior.

History

Abraham Wald coined the term "survivorship bias" in 1941, right as the United States entered World War II to help save the world from an evil dictatorship. Wald, a fugitive from Germany who had lost most of his family in the extermination camps, was a statistician who became involved in the war effort as part of the Statistical Research Group at Columbia University. The SRG was a branch of a nationwide project that enlisted mathematicians to solve intractable problems generals and admirals faced during combat.

One of the most tragic circumstances in the war was the loss of so many B2 bombers over Germany—50 percent never returned to base. The government tasked Wald and his team with how to make the flights safer. Of the airplanes that returned, the military mapped the spots on the plane with the most bullet holes: wing tips, tail, and mid-section. The generals believed those were the areas they must armour; the entire plane could not be armoured or it would not fly. Wald got back to them: "No, you must protect the areas with no bullet holes!" He had deduced that the planes that were shot down had taken fire in the engines, the cockpit, and the tail. The military had only considered the aircraft that survived the missions because they could not assess those that had been lost. The bullet holes in the returning aircraft showed where a bomber could take fire and still fly.

The moral of this story: look for all the things that did *not* happen: the bombers failed to return to base —*why?* Ninety-eight percent of business startups fail —*why?* By looking for the reasons behind the "why," a person will have a much more realistic picture of actual obstacles they must face, and perhaps, like Abraham Wald, they will find clues to help them overcome these obstacles.

2

CONFIRMATION BIAS

Confirmation bias is a habit of thinking that most people adopt or have adopted. A person has set beliefs, certain expectations, or a cherished hypothesis. No matter what evidence they come across that would demolish their way of thinking, they continually refuse to consider it because their original world view is more comfortable for them.

There are so many examples of this bias throughout history and at present that it is surprising human beings have made any progress at all, so widespread is its impact.

Biases and heuristics are similar to one another, and people often confuse them. Heuristics are shortcuts people use when they do not have time to examine every outcome of a decision. Evolutionary psychologists believe heuristics developed as a survival mechanism. I will discuss two of them later on in this book.

Confirmation bias may also be a product of evolution, at least cultural evolution if not genetic, which may be why it is so prevalent. This bias is helpful to people because they experience less stress if they do not have to hold on to totally conflicting ideas, a state of mind called "cognitive dissonance" (see Chapter 15). The stress they experience because of this dissonance might cause them to feel negative emotions, such as anxiety or fear (Segal, D. 2021).

In the United States and many other Western democracies, the right wing and the left have been at odds for decades, and the situation becomes worse every year. This is so true in the US that the populace could not even unite against a common adversary, the coronavirus. Each side has its own media, its own spokespersons, and they rarely tune in to, or read, opinions from the other side. It is just too uncomfortable to contemplate opinions they find abhorrent.

Confirmation Bias Throughout History

Medieval doctors and their heirs through the Age of Enlightenment were history's greatest scam artists. For centuries, they plied their trade on an unsuspecting and trusting public.

Bleeding, purging, cupping, the administration of infusions of every known plant, solutions of every known metal, every conceivable diet including total fasting, most of these based on the weirdest imaginings about the cause of disease, concocted out of nothing but thin air—this was the heritage of medicine up until a little over a century ago (Thomas, 1979, p. 159).

Galen, the famous Greek physician of the ancient world, had already done all the experiments they still relied on. Galen himself encouraged his followers to perform experiments and dissect human bodies, but for 1500 years practitioners aped his work and never expanded on it. If they did experiment, it was only through trial and error. "Cures" that didn't work, had never worked, and that never would work became part of a medical repertoire drawn upon for centuries:

The Case of Dr. Ignaz Semmelweis

Ignaz Semmelweis was born in Hungary in 1818. His father was German, and one can assume his family spoke German, for he travelled to Vienna, Austria, to study medicine. Was he the first doctor to conduct an actual, controlled experiment rather than rely on hit-or-miss methods that then became forever enshrined as procedures in medical practice? Maybe not. But he conducted a valid experiment, with valid results, and the outcome for him and countless suffering women was a disaster.

In 1847, two years after completing his medical training, Dr. Semmelweis got a two-year director's appointment on the maternity wards at a huge teaching hospital in Vienna, the Allgemeine Krankenhaus.

At that hospital and around the world, women who had just given birth were dying at an alarming rate from what people called "childbed fever" (puerperal fever). Dr. Semmelweis studied the situation and made an important observation: women who delivered their babies at the hospital, where the doctors and medical students attended them, were infected and dying at much higher rates (13 to 18 percent mortality rates) than women who delivered at home with the help of midwives or midwife trainees (two percent mortality rate) (Best, M. and Newhauser, D., p. 233).

Dr. Semmelweis considered several hypotheses. He observed that the doctors and medical students often attended births after handling corpses at autopsies and theorized that the doctors and students picked up some infection from the corpses that they then transmitted to their live patients. He noted that midwives had no contact with corpses and concluded that higher mortality rates in hospitals could be mitigated if the doctors and students would wash their hands.

He ordered all the physicians and medical students in his charge to wash their hands in a chloride of lime solution prior to attending a birth, and the mortality rates for patients in his wards fell to two percent, same as the rate for midwife-attended births.

Unfortunately, those doctors on the senior staff (the "old guard") did not take kindly to Semmelweis's innovations. Although many of the younger doctors supported him, he did not get his assistant professorship renewed. This "old guard" believed that a new ventilation system that prevented "miasma" from spreading throughout the hospital and causing infections had reduced childbed fever mortality.

Changing to hand washing would be tough, they thought. It would take too much time when they had so many duties. They would have to install more sinks. Possibly they abhorred the idea because, if they subscribed to it, they would have to admit that *they* caused so many women to die. And everyone knows what egos are like!

Dr. Semmelweis got other appointments to administer maternity wards in Vienna and later back home, in Budapest. With every post, he became more and more strident, ranting against his opponents, calling them murderers. It seemed to the people close to him that he was losing his mind. Eventually, in 1853, his wife committed him to an insane asylum. Someone badly manhandled him while there and he died two years later.

Other Sciences

Confirmation bias is prevalent throughout all the sciences, not only medicine, and this has been the case for centuries. Throughout the years, well-known scientists often reject their peers' discoveries and dismiss out of hand any discovery that appears to disprove a favorite theory. However, the prevalence of the scientific method has made the stubborn stances of individual scientists less damaging than they might have been otherwise. There are checks and balances in science that do not exist among the laity.

Here are a few examples: Galileo would not accept the idea that the moon causes tides to occur throughout the world, a hypothesis first put forward by Kepler. Newton continued to believe the world was only 6,000 years old, despite evidence to the contrary. Other scientists of his day, who could not accept that gravity is a force extending throughout space that cannot be reduced to matter and motion, rejected his theory of universal gravity (Nickerson, R. D., 1998, p. 194).

The examples go on and on in every field of human endeavor: medicine, business, the law, public policy. However, does the prevalence of confirmation bias mean that it has some benefits? The answer is yes. It means that people are far less likely to change their opinions easily and frequently. This tendency leads to more stability within society or within fields of study, and more stability can be a great boon to mental health.

AVAILABILITY HEURISTIC

We often consider the availability bias a heuristic, which is a shortcut people use when making decisions, especially if they do not have the time to study the problem in depth. In the case of the availability heuristic, people estimate whether something is likely to happen based only on examples that come to mind. They are prone to errors doing so because they will think of more remarkable features or events than of everyday examples. Cases of shark attacks may be rare, but they are memorable, so people overestimate the dangers. In other cases, they "massively overweight new information in formulating opinions or making decisions" (Bloom, S., 2021).

Evolutionary psychologists believe this tendency to make snap judgements may be hard-wired into the human brain, a product of millennia when humans constantly faced danger from animals and other tribes, as well as the danger of starving to death, and needed to extract themselves quickly from those sticky situations

Thus, the availability heuristic has its place. It can be useful in extreme situations when time is of the essence; i.e., when people are facing life and death choices. Then, their decisiveness may mean survival. For example, Jews in Germany before World War II only had a couple of years to decide whether to leave. Those who contemplated this decision too long, trying to figure out their odds in a new country vs. remaining in familiar surroundings, paid for their caution with their lives.

Sometimes when people decide based on the most easily accessible information, they rely only on recent information that has made the biggest impression on them. Those memories or facts are easier to recall, whereas other memories and facts take effort and reflection to access them. For example, during the dramatic 2008 recession, the markets receded across the board, but in 2009 stocks bounced back to only ten percent below their value before the crash. But when researchers polled investors about 2009 returns, two-thirds believed the markets had gone down that year. Two thousand and eight had shocked them so greatly that its memories lay uppermost in their minds two years later.

An unlikely example of the availability heuristic is the ubiquitous QWERTY keyboard that typists love to hate. This keyboard layout is a product of bygone years when people used manual typewriters. They fashioned the keyboard that way to keep the more frequently used letters further apart from each other. If someone was typing quickly and hit two of these letters in succession, the letters stuck together, slowing the task down.

In the years since computers became a universal choice for the office or home, various IT technicians have attempted to substitute the QWERTY keyboard with one that is easier to learn and use. But the public is having none of it. They want to keep the familiar keyboard and not have to learn another way to type that might just be easier in the long run.

This age has become known as the Age of Anxiety. People are worried and, with the precipitous spread of the coronavirus, for good reason. But the same black brush does not paint everything. There is good news out there. One trend that has frightened people since Thomas Malthus brought it to the world's attention in 1758 is how populations fluctuate between feast and famine. A country's population grows during good years but then, when it gets too great to feed, people die from famine and the population decreases.

This proposition is so shocking that it has stuck in people's minds even after many years. However, studies show that the world's population is leveling off. The most recent year that population grew the fastest is 1968, and birth rates have decreased dramatically every year since then. The reason the world's population is continuing to grow now is because people are living longer. Jack Bobo (2020) writes that "by the end of the 21st century the global population will likely begin to decline."

Climate Change and the "Unavailability Heuristic"

The decisions made because of the availability heuristic are products of the human brain's fertile imagination. Imagining the horror of a shark attack makes the danger seem more real and more prevalent than is the case. But is there an "unavailabity" heuristic? Richard Lazarus (2009) believes there is. When writing an article for the *Cornell Law Review* in which he considers how the law deals with "wicked problems," particularly climate change, Lazarus describes how seemingly inviolable environmental laws become weakened when succeeding administrations cannot adjust budgets, write needed legislation, or simply enforce the laws.

One issue he believes contributes to the degradation of these laws is the failure by people to comprehend fully the danger we all face. Policy makers have expressed the fear that the availability heuristic will cause laws to be written to cover events that loom large in the human imagination, yet are quite rare. Thus, they believe the heuristic may lead to overregulation.

However, Lazarus believes that with climate change, exactly the opposite is occurring:

Climate change, however, most implicates the mirror image of the availability heuristic. There is no reason to suppose that the availability heuristic's only policy implication is the tendency to overregulate. Just as problems that can be easily imagined may in theory prompt overregulation, problems that cannot be easily imagined—and therefore presumably implicate an "unavailability heuristic"—may be plagued by under-regulation. Climate change, of course, is just such an unimaginable problem.

Lazarus points to several reasons it is so hard for people to imagine the true impact of climate change. First is its spatial dimension. It is happening in every corner of the globe and its causes and effects spread far and wide. The consequences of climate change lack "immediacy in space," so people are uncertain about its exact impact in a distant location. Far away consequences make them invisible and more abstract. Also, people do not really understand the science behind climate change and so they react intuitively to the threat through the availability heuristic.

Not only are the effects of climate change in far-off places often dramatically different from those near home, but the nations likely to suffer the least, at least in the short term, often bear responsibility for its cataclysmic effects on other nations.

Another study analyzed why European nations issue more regulations to combat climate change than does the United States. The researchers found that two unconscious mechanisms were in play: the availability heuristic and confirmation bias (Chapters 2 and 3). For Europeans, the availability heuristic makes them favor more stringent environmental regulation because the confirmation bias renders them more disposed to favor this course. They are more willing to pay for environmental mitigation than many Americans, who often oppose environmental controls. These different predispositions cause the confirmation bias to kick in, and that affects how the availability heuristic plays out in the different cultures regarding climate change (Sunstein, C.).

Countering the Availability Heuristic in Daily Life

People who make mistakes on account of the availability heuristic are often people in a hurry. The best thing they can do to counteract this tendency is to consciously slow down so their brains can catch up. It is interesting to note that our brains can receive significantly more bits of information a second than it can consciously process. In the conclusion to this book, I discuss fast and slow thinking as described by the famous psychologist, Daniel Kahneman. Kahneman, along with his partner, Amos Tversky, first described and researched many of the biases discussed in this book What may be his final work,

Thinking, Fast and Slow, was on the *New York Times'* bestsellers list in 2011, the year he published it.

Other ways to counter the heuristic are simple pieces of advice, such as taking a walk, sleeping on it, coming up with checklists; and doing whatever you have to do to gain a better perspective on your problem. And, as so many have pointed out, pay attention to your health. Despite shocking videos of car crashes, statistics show that many more people die from heart attacks than from auto accidents.

Availability bias has a purpose—to remember something that is surprising or horrifying more easily than everyday narratives. That way, people can be on the lookout for potential future dangers. However, these days, the bias can pose a problem because people affected by it misjudge the probability of a thing happening or the frequency with which it will happen.

4

LOSS AVERSION BIAS (PROSPECT THEORY)

Loss aversion bias is similar to the sunk cost fallacy, discussed in Chapter 10, in that people are averse to cutting their losses. In the aversion bias's case, for most people, the pain of losing is so acute that it can be twice as powerful as the pleasure one feels at winning. Prior to findings published by famed behavioral scientists Amos Tversky and Daniel Kahneman, economists all thought that humans are rational actors. Humans should feel as much pain when they lose $100 as they feel pleasure when they gain $100. But Tversky and Kahneman proved this to be untrue.

The investment community knows loss aversion well. One of the first questions a financial planner will ask a client is how much risk they will take when making investments. Very often people avoid risky investments despite the chance they might make a great more money than if they invested in safer companies. Therefore, advisors caution that, if you want to make money in the stock market, do so with money you can afford to lose.

Loss aversion also comes into play in marketing situations, wherein marketers offer free trials or rebates in order to get people to buy their product. People would like to believe they are getting something for free. But, when they actually start using the "free" service or product, their aversion to loss often makes them decide to buy it so they will not have to feel they have lost something when they have to give it up. Actually, scaling back, on trials of products or software, nice cars, or larger houses, is a tough decision for most people, who find the ensuing feeling of loss emotionally challenging.

The loss aversion bias can deeply affect how people come to financial decisions, and often negatively. Maybe a person knows they need to downsize but puts it off so long they find creditors knocking at their door or have to file for bankruptcy, often a precarious step on a downward economic spiral.

What Loss Aversion Can Mean for the Planet

Loss aversion can affect large institutions, companies, and countries. When researchers find newer, better ways, more environmentally sensitive ways to solve endemic problems like climate change, often loss aversion stands in the way as the biggest barrier to progress and, not only progress, the future of the world as well. It is probable that most oil companies have enough funds to produce environmentally cleaner energy, but they consistently lobby against these changes. Board members and executives consider the billions already invested in oil and gas drilling and distribution and want to continue producing energy as they did in the past.

Farmers are often stubborn folk, hard set in their ways, whether in the developed world or in the developing one. When the government of Brazil encouraged its scientists to work on ways to reduce the mosquito population responsible for so much disease in the tropics, their scientists discovered how to genetically modify the mosquitoes so that the mosquito population became all male, unable to reproduce. Many countries adopted this newer method that was so much better for the environment, but European countries continued to rely on insecticides. Loss aversion in their agricultural sectors made them hesitant to try new methods of combating insect pests.

Why Loss Aversion Occurs

Three separate and distinct factors make loss aversion a feature of our human makeup: neurological processes, cultural background, and socioeconomic conditions.

The first process occurs in the brain's amygdala, which deeply correlates loss with fear. People experience almost automated anxiety when exposed to certain animals, like snakes or spiders, or when they experience turbulence if traveling by plane.

There is also a part of the brain that helps humans avoid future losses by helping them become better predictors. MRI scans of this part, called the striatum, show it lights up when a person experiences both gains and losses, but it lights up more when they experience losses.

And then there is a part of the brain that reacts to the emotion of disgust and works with the amygdala so that individuals automatically avoid certain types of behavior. This area, the inula, lights up during an MRI scan as an individual responds to a loss. The higher the probability of loss, the more activated the inula becomes, especially when compared to an equivalent gain (The Decision Lab).

The cultural and socioeconomic factors behind loss aversion essentially depend on where an individual is born and their circumstances.

Wealthy and powerful individuals are far less loss averse than less privileged individuals in their society simply because they have more resources to cushion any losses they might incur.

Regarding cultural conditions, people from individualist societies are more loss averse than those from collectivist cultures. That means people from Africa are far less loss averse than people from Eastern Europe, for example, because Africans mostly enjoy far more social connections they can rely on when, or if, they experience problems because of financial decisions they have made.

Prospect Theory and the Iranian Hostage Rescue Mission

Prospect theory is a way to analyze people's aversion to losses in contrast to their attraction to gains when every choice available risks a loss. The theory considers the value a person places on an option ("value function") and the objective likelihood that an outcome will occur ("weighting function").

In February 1980, when Iranian militants captured the U.S. Embassy in Tehran and took everyone there hostage, President Jimmy Carter faced the worst crisis of his administration. Relations with Iran were already rocky after the Islamist revolution, and militant students had taken the embassy only a few months before. Iranian officials, who had intervened in the first embassy takeover, now refused to negotiate with Carter's emissaries.

Because of this situation, U.S. prestige abroad was more on the line than ever, and Carter's popularity on the home front was sinking fast. His reelection campaign was going to be tough.

The choices facing him were: 1) war with Iran; 2) more sanctions on Iran; and 3) a rescue mission.

When looked at through the lens of prospect theory, the failed April 1980 rescue mission, resulting in the death of eight American soldiers and two civilians, was the best choice. War would have been militarily riskier than the rescue mission, and war did not guarantee the safe release of the hostages. If Carter limited his response to imposing further sanctions on Iran, he risked further erosion of his approval rating among the American public. And increased sanctions would not guarantee the rescue of the hostages and might make their situation far worse. Therefore, his choice, although bad, was the best among options that appeared to be worse (McDermott, R., 1998).

Carter's actions revealed the truth of a theory that political leaders will not undertake bold and politically risky initiatives when they are most powerful. Instead, they undertake riskier policies when they are at their most vulnerable (Weyland, K., 2002). This is certainly true of President Carter's situation. He was in danger of losing his reelection bid and, in fact, he did lose it.

5

HINDSIGHT BIAS

Having the "benefit of hindsight" is a common observation often heard in conversation when people are discussing person A's opinion of a past event. The people say that person A stated an opinion about an event in the past person A "knew" was going to happen when, at the time of the event, person A actually did not know this event would occur.

Person A has been guilty of hindsight bias. They have attempted to increase their self-esteem by presenting themselves as more perceptive than they actually were. This often occurs when they had spotted an opportunity but failed to take advantage of it because they *were* unsure. For example, they spot a stock going for only a dollar a share. They think it will go up, but at the time they cannot decide to buy it. Then, when in a few weeks they see the stock is selling at two dollars a share, they say "I *knew* it would go up!" when they did not know.

Hindsight bias is extremely common, and most people have likely displayed it. In one study, researchers asked participants to predict the outcome of a Senate vote. Fifty-eight percent responded that the vote would pass. Then, the bill passed, and they asked the same participants if they had thought it would. Now, 80 percent said they thought it would pass. Hindsight bias distorted many participants' perception of how they had really felt prior to the Senate vote.

Hindsight bias can lead to overconfidence because it leads people to believe that they knew things all along, even though the future is inherently unknowable and no one can predict what will happen with one hundred percent accuracy. If someone tells themselves enough times that they have always been right and uses their so-called insights to impress others, they can start believing it themselves. If a person consistently believes they are always right and that they had indeed predicted future events, their efforts at decision making may turn out disastrously.

Hindsight bias can lead a person down a primrose path because there are three levels to this delusion. First off is *memory distortion,* when we only believe we thought it would happen. Here, a person's recollection of a past event is skewed. A person recalls their previous thoughts and believes that they had predicted an event prior to it occurring. The memories seem certain, etched in our minds in black and white.

In this way, hindsight bias helps our brain

"process the world around us. By doing so, the event that occurred starts to make more sense"

— (BOYCE, P. 2020)

Memory distortion can lead to a feeling that the event was *inevitable* as we try to make sense of why it happened. We say to ourselves, "It had to happen."

Here, the forces of cause and effect come into play when we misinterpret the cause and posit the wrong reason for the effect. Now we are living in a fictional universe instead of the real one.

The sense that the event was inevitable builds upon memory distortion, as the person exaggerates their previous beliefs. This can be a coping mechanism in highly controlled situations that are win or lose. For example, the losers in a foot race will tell themselves, "I never had a chance," whereas, in reality, at the beginning of the race, they thought their chances of winning were good. This helps them cope with the pain of losing. They can keep their self-esteem and make sense of the situation at the same time.

The last stop is *foreseeability*, when we say to ourselves, "I knew it would happen." If the outcome seems like it was foreseeable, that means that we had control, understood the situation, and predicted the result.

Did we know it would happen because of our superior intelligence? Knowledge? Expertise? We have just given a boost to our self-esteem while sacrificing the truth. This type of thinking alleviates our feelings of lack of control in uncertain times (Boyce, P. 2020).

Hindsight Bias, the Press, and Covid-19

In early December 2020, when reporters in China first exposed the Covid-19 outbreak in Wuhan, stories about it in the Western press mainly focused on the Chinese government's draconian measures in locking down Wuhan province. They exposed human rights abuses but expressed no fear about what this meant for the rest of the world. Certain experts had predicted the onset of a worldwide pandemic, but their concerns never made it into the mainstream press.

Reporters and the public saw it as another localized disease, like the Middle East Respiratory Syndrome outbreak in the Arabian Peninsula in 2012, that posed a minor threat to other countries. Later that December, "Severe Acute Respiratory Syndrome Coronavirus 2," or SARS-CoV-2, the virus's scientific name, came trickling in, at first, before it struck like a roaring lion.

Later, a year later, most stories focused in hindsight on countries' unpreparedness for the pandemic, especially in the United States. We knew it was coming, so why didn't we do something about it?

This is an example of the press in entire cultures latching onto the hindsight bias to gain purchase on a deadly, ever-changing, and devastating situation and emerge with some sense of control over it.

6

ANCHORING BIAS (PRIMING)

The anchoring bias is about unconscious strategies that immediately take place when a person faces making a decision. With no other information to go on, the person latches onto the first piece of information that they had about the problem. Then they often stick with that information despite new data. Also, if another person asks them for a decision and provides a number that could represent the answer, the respondent's answers are skewed to reflect that number because it was the first number they got to solve the problem.

A well-known study showing how important these first impressions are asked two groups of people at what age Mahatma Gandhi died. To introduce the question, the investigator provided both groups with numbers that on their face made little sense. For one group, he asked if Gandhi died before or after the age of nine, and, for the second group, he asked if the world-renowned leader died before or after the age of 140. The group given the lower number, "nine" guessed Gandhi died at age 50. The group given a top age of 140 guessed he died at 67. Both were incorrect, as the sage died at 87, when he was assassinated. The second group reacted to the higher anchor number (the first piece of information provided) to give an age that more closely approximated the correct answer. The first group decided Gandhi had died younger because the researchers had given them a lower number.

What this also shows is that the "anchor" was a number, a number that made little sense but still made a critical impression on the minds of the participants. In most examples, anchors are numbers, perhaps because they are so precise and leave little to the imagination.

Another example that shows just how illogical this process is is when people wrote the last two digits of their Social Security number (in the US) and then were shown a box of chocolate. Those who had a higher number said they would pay more for the chocolates than those with lower numbers. This was true even though they realized there is no relationship between social security numbers and chocolate, and also true even if they were aware of the anchoring bias.

The anchoring bias has its purpose: to help humans make calculated guesses on answers they do not know when nothing else is at hand to support a more accurate answer. For example, if they do not know the exact date the Pilgrims landed at Plymouth Rock but know the century, they can guess it is sometime early in the 17th century and answer a multiple-choice test correctly where one answer is December 1620.

The Anchoring Bias in Salary Negotiations

A bit of advice often geared toward people about to engage in salary negotiations is not to advance any kind of preliminary figure, no matter how many times the interviewer asked. The thinking is that people can only hurt themselves by giving the preliminary number because if it is too high, the interviewer will just say "you are high," and the person will lose money. If the number they give is low, the interviewer will say nothing, and they will still lose money.

However, those who have studied the anchoring bias say this strategy is the wrong approach. Instead, making the first offer works in the interviewee's favor. Instead, when negotiating, it is best to advance a figure the interviewee thinks might be unrealistic but serves as a set point for the salary they will eventually receive.

This approach worked when a professor from the University of Idaho tested it on university students, whom he asked to come up with a starting salary for a fictitious female applicant, who, they all were told, had earned $29,000 per year at her last job.

One group of students read a statement by the interviewee which said, "Well, I'd like $100,000, but really I am just looking for something that is fair." The control group did not have this statement, and they proposed a salary of $32,463. However, the group who knew that the candidate put the number $100,000 out there, though she said she only wanted what is fair, proposed a salary of $35,523. A difference of over three thousand dollars, resulting in a nine percent higher salary, is no small change (Karawynn, 2012).

The candidate threw out the $100,000 in jest, but she still got a higher salary.

The other way to accomplish this goal is to research salary ranges for that line of work and name a number near the top.

People using either method must be sure to state their preferences with confidence, no matter how anxious they may actually feel. They can build up the needed confidence by finding someone with whom to rehearse. They could try tossing off a few high salary jokes, such as:

What sort of salary are you looking for?

"Well, I'm looking for a million dollars, but I suppose you could convince me to take a little less than that if the job were really awesome."

What is the minimum salary you would accept?

"*One point five million and not a penny less.*"

What are your salary requirements?

"*Three hundred thousand dollars, full family health premiums, and a 10% 401(k) match. And a pony*"

— (KARAWYNN, 2012)

Anchoring Bias and the Consumer

When in the market for a car, a person who is at the dealership to negotiate a price should realize the preliminary figure the salesperson provides will have an oversized impact on the price they will eventually pay. To combat this bias, they should do their homework and come to the meeting prepared with a spectrum of prices backed up by data. A salesperson could engage a customer in long-term dickering over the price they first named but, when they finally reach a lower figure the customer feels good about, it turns out that is a price the salesperson wanted to sell the car for all along.

The same situation is in play for every other product on the market. For example, when a person visits a furniture store and tells the sales clerk they want a sofa, it is likely the salesperson will lead them straight to a couch costing one thousand dollars or more.When they say they want something a little cheaper, the clerk then leads them to a sofa priced at $700. When they balk at that price, the salesclerk leads them to a clearance item, on sale for "only $650). By now this seems like a good deal, so they purchase it. They never find out until later that right next door to the high-end furniture store is one selling items that fall within the price range they had in mind.

Prices of items on sale can be quite deceptive. Usually, whether online or in the store, they also list the former price of the object in question. That is the anchor price, and that is the price that convinces the consumer they got a good deal. Unfortunately, often the customer has no way of knowing if the former price was really the former price, or if it was just made up for the occasion.

Real estate agents set up anchors when a person wants to rent a house. At first they show their customers run-down properties with rents set very high. It is when their client is sadly realizing that they cannot afford to rent a nice house that the agent shows them a decent property. The rent is twenty-five percent higher than the rents of the objectionable properties, but at that point, the prospective renter believes they have a good deal.

Market Forecasts

Consensus forecasts are predictions of future market prices and are based on multiple sources, which are then averaged to come up with what fore-casters hope is a realistic figure. The Federal Reserve

Board in 2007 wanted to know how accurate these forecasts are because they might affect market prices.

Specifically, the Board wondered if these published "forecasts of monthly economic releases from Money Market Services surveys from 1990 to 2006 have a tendency to be systematically biased toward the value of previous months' data releases" (Campbell, S. D. and Sharpe, S. A.). This study found evidence of anchoring, meaning that the forecasts were biased in favor of the previous months' data. However, the study also found that the market insiders following this news anticipated the influence of anchoring. Therefore, the behavioral bias did not influence how they predicted interest rates or make the market more volatile, the report concluded (Campbell, S. D. and Sharpe, S. A.).

British Troops on Cyprus in WWII and the Anchoring Bias

In war, the British military have often proved themselves masters of deception. Think of the movie, *The Imitation Game* (2014), wherein scientists recruited by the military unraveled secret German codes throughout the entirety of World War II with the help of a primitive, but totally operational, computer they built themselves. In another example of ingenuous deception, the British military took advantage of the anchoring bias to fool the Germans about British troop strength.

This deception was just as elaborate as that in *The Imitation Game,* but quite different in its execution. It exploited the bias on many levels. The British worried that their 4000 troops on the island of Cyprus were too few to ward off an attack by the Germans. If the Germans thought there were 20,000 troops there instead of 4000, they probably would not attack, they theorized. They then set about to establish an illusion of a larger number of troops through varied means. First, they created false division headquarters and barracks on the island. This "headquarters" even had its own fleet of jeeps. They also transmitted phony radio messages from a fake division commander that the Germans intercepted. As a final touch, they came up with fake defensive plans with maps and false orders, passed on to the Germans via double agents and the ruse of a lost briefcase.

The Germans fell for the 20,000 number and never wavered from that belief for the rest of the war, even though they later had access to good information that refuted it. This is how powerful the anchoring bias can be (Williams, B. S., 2020).

Anchoring Bias and the Law

In the United States, judges can exercise their discernment when sentencing someone found guilty of breaking the law. However, the judge usually considers the prosecutors' and attorneys' recommendations. In certain cases, a probation officer recommends a sentence. According to research, these recommendations heavily influenced judges because they serve as anchors influencing the final decision.

In a study, the researchers provided two different anchoring numbers to several criminal court judges. For some in the group, the recommended sentence was a mere two months, while for the others, the recommendations were 34 months for the same crime. The judges wrote about how appropriate the sentence was, and then they said what they would impose.

The anchor numbers significantly affected the length of sentences. When averaged, judges who had the lower recommendation said the defendant should serve 19.78 months, while the judges given the higher anchor said 28.7 months (The Decision Lab).

Settlement Negotiations

A typical settlement negotiation is a personal injury case where the injured party sues for damages. In these cases, the initial positions are advanced by the injured party. To take advantage of the anchoring bias, claimants usually advance a settlement figure higher than the true cost of their claim.

Lawyers for the defense best counter this not by low-balling and presenting an absurdly low figure, but by making a convincing argument that the amount the defendant will pay is the correct amount. They must come to the negotiating table armed with data to support their position.

These lawyers also have to watch out for other biases, such as decision escalation, which is when the parties base a current decision on past actions and ignore newer, relevant information. Or, they might be so committed to settling the dispute that they continue to escalate their offers (Kern, G., 2019).

Since the anchoring effect is unconscious, it is impossible to avoid completely. However, people can mitigate its effects by weighing reasons the anchor does not fit the situation.

How Can People Avoid the Anchoring Bias?

The sad truth is, they cannot. Everyone is susceptible to it. Tests of students and experts to reveal how much experts could shake off the bias as compared to nonexperts showed the experts responded not much better than the hoi polloi. So, when heading to the store or to an online site, people must realize the retailer is always trying to get them to pay a higher price.

If the prospective customer waits to consider their options, they may be less susceptible to the bias. Exploring options might mean comparing the most expensive and least expensive models to decide if the higher price is justified. A person who has some knowledge about the cost of what they want may set a mental anchor before going into a store. It may be useful to explore online to arrive at what the average price is for a certain model and to delay decisions until after exploring five options.

Dropping Anchor

For negotiators hoping to make a good deal, knowledge is key, especially concerning the "zone of possible agreement." This is the range of options that both sides will find acceptable. Of course, the negotiator knows their own zone, but what about the other side? This is where research can be really helpful—in fact necessary, because this knowledge will help the person confidently make an aggressive first offer and expect that their offer will be to their advantage and anchor the negotiation.

If the other side "drops anchor" first, that figure must be dealt with prior to making a counteroffer with a statement like: "I'm not trying to play games with you, but we are miles apart on price." Then they should move fast and throw out their counterproposal. One thing not to do is mention the offered price (the anchor) because that would validate it. After countering, they should explain why it is a fair price (Shonk, K., 2021).

7

EGOCENTRIC BIAS

As its name implies, the egocentric bias is a cognitive bias that predisposes a person to favor their own outlook on life and also causes them to imagine others are looking at them and/or thinking about them when such is not the case. It is an unconscious bias that comes into play, even when someone is actively trying to understand another person's perspective. This bias makes people underestimate how different another person's viewpoint is from their own or to ignore completely another's point of view.

The egocentric bias works to either inflate a person's ideas about their own importance or to undermine their self-confidence because, when they make a mistake or do something embarrassing, they assume others are as aware of these gaffes as they are. For example, someone who feels nervous while speaking in public assumes that their nervousness is clear to the audience because it is so apparent to them.

When a person holds treasured beliefs, they struggle to imagine how other people could believe something completely different. This bias becomes pronounced in the areas of politics or religion. A person cannot imagine why a family member or a neighbor is not as passionate about a political candidate as they are. The egocentric bias can thus cause deep rifts between people who previously and liked or loved one another.

Of course, the bias comes through clearly in present-day conflicts where another person's political beliefs come under scrutiny and found wanting. And it can make for very uncomfortable holiday dinners.

In the workplace, the egocentric bias can cause a person to overestimate their contributions to a project's success and to underplay their responsibilities for its failure. This can hold true for present endeavors and also for past accomplishments, when a person inaccurately remembers their actual role in events. They remember themselves as key players, when actually they played only a minor part.

A psychological diagnosis called "projection" can originate in a person's unconscious egocentric bias. In such cases, people project their own emotions, beliefs, desires and thoughts onto others, especially on people who are close to them. A person who projects a lot of their "stuff" onto other people obviously lacks empathy for what others might be feeling. Thus, they just ignore those feelings and remain ignorant of what is going on around them.

Another way the egocentric bias affects our lives is that it can cause people to believe a situation is fair when it is helpful to them, while, if the situation were reversed, they would think it was unfair that others had these advantages. This bias becomes very clear when advocates for racial justice talk about White privilege, and many Whites profess not to understand the concept.

Similarly, while people believe they deserve more than others when splitting positive outcomes, they can also believe they deserve less than others when negative outcomes must be apportioned.

The Whys and Wherefores of the Egocentric Bias

The egocentric bias occurs because the brain relies on shortcuts, or heuristics, to quickly and easily form judgements. These heuristics, such as the anchor bias discussed in Chapter 6, and others like the availability bias, also discussed in this book (Chapter 3) are oversimplified evaluations of situations that are based on experience and/or learned from others (Lesage, D. 2019).

Evolutionary psychologists believe these manners of decision-making have been hard-wired into our brains. As with other types of evolution that do not involve cognition, the process develops because it is good enough, considering the energy involved and time constraints required for deciding (Wu, Bozhi, 2019).

Specifically, the egocentric bias exists because we mostly look at the world from our perspective. Therefore, when we remember events, we remember them primarily from our point of view. So, when we decide it is necessary to examine an issue from another person's point of view, *"we tend to anchor this new perspective to our own, and so we often fail to adjust from our original viewpoint enough to properly assess situations"*

— (EFFECTIVIOLOGY)

Because we usually rely on heuristics to decide, our brains are going to search for the easiest and fastest way. The easiest way, most times, is to just assume other people think like we do. Our brains want to evade all the mental footwork involved in truly evaluating another person's outlook.

In recalling past events, people see them through the lens of the egocentric bias because our brains arrange our memories around ourselves. Our presence at these moments in the past is a constant, the center of our attention most of the time.

Many factors explain why a person is behaving out of an egocentric bias. Age can be one: older adults and children are more likely to use it. Also, bilingual or multi-lingual persons have less egocentric bias, perhaps because they have studied other cultures in depth along with their language learning. Researchers have even detected differences among people depending on the type of fiction they read. Those who read genre fiction have more of an egocentric bias than those who read literary fiction (Castano, C., Martingano, A. J., Perconti, P., 2020).

Stereotyping Welfare Recipients

A study of consumers and their particular food preferences showed that these attitudes about food contributed to an overall egocentric bias against welfare recipients and the welfare system (Shepherd S. and Campbell T., 2020). The researchers found that when a welfare recipient bought an item that a participant did not value, the participant stereotyped those on welfare more than they had before as lazy, irresponsible, and impulsive. Their attitude did not change when the researchers told them about positive qualities the welfare recipient displayed, such as sticking to a budget, making lists, or clipping coupons. The researchers concluded personal preferences play an outsized role in people's attitudes toward the welfare system, and they connected these attitudes to the egocentric bias, which they said was robust (Shepherd, S. and Campbell, T., 2020).

Is There a Way to Counteract Egocentrism?

Four ways to counteract the bias were mentioned by *Effectiviogy*: develop awareness of the bias, use self-distancing language, consider alternative viewpoints, and slow down your reasoning process to make it more explicit. Self-distancing means trying to think about yourself in the second or third person, such as asking yourself: "how much did you contribute to the project?" or using your own name, such as "how much did John contribute to the project?"

One way to increase self-awareness is to sit in front of a mirror while deciding.

When thinking of alternative viewpoints, try to visualize a problem, such as a quarrel with a friend, from their perspective instead of yours. Or, consider arguments that contradict your existing opinions. Or, actually talk to people (calmly!) who hold opposing viewpoints. Also, when deciding, consider how to account for someone's egocentric bias on that topic.

The *Effectivology* authors warn we cannot reduce the egocentric bias in all situations. In fact, these measures only help reduce the bias in some degree or other, because this bias is resistant to change. Also, a person who thinks they have reduced their biases without outside verification may actually make poor decisions because they are now over-confident.

8

PYGMALION EFFECT BIAS

Some college students volunteered to take part in an experiment run by well-known psychologist and professor, Robert Rosenthal. Rosenthal did not tell his students beforehand the purpose of the experiment. He divided them into two groups and gave each group some rats for testing. He told the first group that they had very special rats, very intelligent ones that probably were superior genetically to the rats the second group of students were testing. In contrast, the second group of students were told that their rats were unexceptional and, in fact, might be genetically disadvantaged. However, the professor had picked the rats randomly and had measured no differences between the two groups of rats.

The students who had the "superior" rats treated their animals affectionately, but the students with the so-called "inferior" rats paid little attention to their subjects and showed them no warmth or affection.

Rosenthal found his hypothesis held true. He believed people live up to high expectations and prove negative expectations true by their own actions and behavior. His students had held high expectations of the "smarter" rats and had treated them well. These animals performed the last task, which both groups of rats had to complete, admirably. The rats that students had treated badly and expected little of did poorly. Some were so discouraged they never left the starting line.

Later, in 1968, Rosenthal and a collaborator, high school principal Lenore Jacobson, published a book that got a lot of attention in the educational and psychological communities: *Pygmalion in the Classroom.* They called their thesis the "self-fulfilling prophecy." Now the subjects were primary school children, not rats, but, like the rats before them, they proved the original hypothesis: behavior, either animal or human, appears to align with what others expect of them.

The Pygmalion effect got its name from a mythic Greek king who was also a sculptor. Pygmalion fell in love with one of his creations, Galatea. When Galatea came to life after Pygmalion entreated Athena for a wife that looked like his statue, he married her. This, at least, was the Greek poet Ovid's version of the myth.

A more modern version by George Bernard Shaw is probably the model that gave the Pygmalion effect its name. In this play, *Pygmalion*, Profession Higgins brings a girl to "life" by teaching her proper manners and speech so that she can be" socially acceptable."

The Pygmalion effect is also called the Rosenthal and Jacobson effect.

The Oak School Experiment

In Rosenthal and Jacobson's Oak School experiment (actually Spruce School, located just south of San Francisco), at the start of the school year the researchers drew up a random list of 20 percent of the children enrolled there and then informed their teachers that these particular children had great potential for learning. They then tested all students in the school for IQ. Eight months later, they tested the students again.

Eight months later, these unusual or "magic" children showed significantly greater gains in IQ than did the remaining children who had gotten little of the teachers' attention. The change in the teachers' expectations regarding the intellectual performance of these allegedly "special" children had led to an actual change in the intellectual performance of these randomly selected children (Rosenthal, R,. and Jacobson, L., 1968,pp. VI-VII).

In the first part of their book, Rosenthal and Jacobson discuss the poor educational outcomes of lower-class children at the time of the study and the importance to the nation that their performance improve. They point to technological improvements reflected in the workplace that children from lower-class backgrounds could not master.

The government was spending vast amounts of money on education, but if educational outcomes did not improve, all the effort expended and money spent would be wasted. This is even more the case today. At present, we cannot fill millions of jobs, often because the people educated to fill these jobs do not exist.

Rosenthal and Jacobson discuss the self-fulfilling prophecy from psychological, medical, and sociological perspectives. This all led up to what they believed was the most important issue in education and one that must change for lower-class children to succeed: teacher expectation is a factor in this mix that Rosenthal and others thought could change.

However, experiments done in succeeding years have shown that this change does not come about easily, if at all. What these later experiments have shown is that teachers' expectations that certain of their students are going to succeed brilliantly have to emanate from the teachers' subconscious. The teachers cannot know ahead of time much about their students' background and abilities—they have to be tricked into having those high expectations of some of their students.

More recent studies have centered on how to work around such mental barriers. Some teacher training modules that give aspiring teachers video feedback showing some unconscious traits and facial expressions, which students might interpret as discouraging or encouraging, have resulted in excellent outcomes in the classroom. The work on how to overcome the self-fulling prophecy and rekindle the Pygmalion magic thus continues.

9

HALO EFFECT BIAS

Reminding people how important first impressions are is not only excellent advice, but the existence of the halo bias proves its truth. This is a cognitive bias that can work in both positive and negative ways.

Often, a person who makes a good first impression can do no wrong in the eyes of people who formed that excellent opinion practically on first sight. Movie stars often experience this sort of adulation. Their admirers view them as perfect, and the stars have publicists who try to keep any of the stars' stickier escapades and destructive habits out of the public eye.

This halo effect works well for them, even when the news is bad. Their fans refuse to believe it and even when it is absolutely true. Consider Hugh Grant's unsavory dalliance with prostitutes. The charming star emerged almost untouched by the scandal.

The golden aura of the halo effect just seems to work for some, but not others. Donald Trump had at least two, if not more, affairs before his nomination, but that made no difference to his core supporters. But politicians like Gary Hart have had their careers ended when rumors of an illicit romance proved true.

The above examples show the importance of looks in the halo effect equation. But also traits like charisma and charm work their way into the mix. It is thus difficult to predict who will win or who will lose in the court of public opinion.

The Halo Effect in the Workplace

The halo effect can mean that the first impression we make affects people's perception of almost every-thing we do down the road. In the workplace, our future success may depend on our first contact with prospective employers. The human brain works extremely fast when forming judgements: about one-tenth of a second! An individual's attractiveness ranked high in a Princeton study of how people judged faces with respect to competence, intelligence, and likeability (Wargo, E., 2006).

During an interview, the halo effect can work positively or negatively. If positive, the candidate's next words are judged favorably, but if negative, the person has little chance to improve upon that undesirable impression.

The halo effect, being biased toward attractiveness, has little to do with a person's ability to accomplish the task at hand, and so HR recruiters often receive training on how to recognize this bias in themselves and account for it in their decisions. If this does not occur, employees in that company will often feel resentment that some can advance when actually others not so advantaged have completed a job in the same way or even better. The company may even single out employees not so favored for harsher discipline. Also, if the company believes one employee is more valuable in one area, it still might ignore their deficiencies in other areas, which is bad for the company down the line if they promote people who lack some competencies needed to do an effective job, provide a good example, and be a good team leader (Miller, B., 2018).

The Halo Effect at School

In primary school, everybody hates the "teacher's pet," but students either compete for that special status or rebel against the whole idea of school because they perceive the teacher's habit of picking favorites to be unfair and know they will never have the chance to shine in that teacher's eyes.

On the first days of class after the teacher grades an assignment, the teacher often sees the students who handed in an A paper in such a positive light that these students sometimes continue to get top grades even if their work turns sloppy. The teacher just expects these students to continue to produce high-quality work. Conversely, the teacher will have low expectations of students who initially handed in poorer work and will continue to skew their grades downward, even though the student later produces work equal to or better than that of the students enjoying the positive halo effect. We often call this the "horns" or "devil" effect.

As Anissimov writes,

"Because our entire lives are permeated by these cognitive judgments, studies of biases like the halo effect go down to the very fabric that underlies our society."

— ANISSIMOV

When commanding officers rated their soldiers, they strongly correlated positive and negative qualities with one another.

" This shows that people paint others with a broad brush— 'good in general' or 'bad in general' "

— (ANISSIMOV, M.)

This tendency to leap to such quick judgements has an anchoring effect that lasts long after a superior judges one of their subordinates, despite studies that have shown that past behavior predicts future behavior much better than interviewer impressions (Anissimov, M.).

Everyone makes judgements that involve the halo effect bias, every day of their lives. It is an unconscious reaction so pervasive its cultural impact is almost impossible to measure. People struggle against it if they have been subject to the "horns" effect, and see their privileges as well-deserved should they have been so fortunate as to have their lives influenced by the halo effect. The best way to counter these reactions is to become conscious of how we judge others.

10

DECISION FATIGUE BIAS

Decision fatigue bias is common when people who have been deciding all day make poor decisions or at least not optimal decisions by the end of the day because they feel overwhelmed by all the choices they still have to make. In one well-known example, President Obama wore the same color suit every day to reduce the cognitive burden on his brain from having to make so many decisions. This was one decision, at least, that he did not have to worry about.

No matter how intelligent or how skilled, everyone can experience decision fatigue because of mental exhaustion. The brain takes illogical shortcuts to help the decision-making process. Except what the brain does is not helpful because the shortcuts result in decisions that are less deliberative. The person has not taken the time to make a good decision. Or, the person procrastinates and puts off a potentially important decision requiring immediate attention until tomorrow, or next week, or some other time in the future.

Decision Fatigue and Poverty

A person's economic background often affects their decision-making abilities. Poverty-stricken people simply face more decisions than wealthier individuals. This is because they must make many trade-offs during a typical day that a wealthier person does not have to consider. For example, at the grocery store they might have to decide between buying eggs or milk because they do not have enough money for both products, but the richer person simply buys both products if the products are on their list of things to buy.

How this plays out is if a poor person must make these trade-off decisions day after day, they then have less mental energy to devote to other crucial aspects in their lives like their job or looking for work and devoting sufficient time to school work. Decision fatigue may leave them trapped in poverty because they could not dedicate themselves fully to the activities that would afford them chances to better their odds of attaining middle class status and leading a more comfortable and fulfilling life.

The effect of decision fatigue on poverty was first documented in a study conducted at 20 villages in Rajasthan, India, by economist Dean Spears from Princeton University. Dean tested how the fatigue from deciding to buy soap at a steeply discounted price affected villagers' willpower through giving them various tasks and later compared the poorer villagers' responses with those of people from more affluent villages (The Decision Lab).

Theory and Origins

Social psychologist Roy E. Baumeister first coined the term "decision fatigue" when describing the mental and emotional strain resulting from having to make multiple choices, but Sigmund Freud had already written about a state he called "ego depletion." Freud developed a mental energy model and theorized that a person's ego depends on mental activities requiring a transfer of energy. His theory of a mental energy model went mainly unnoticed until Baumeister's experiments showed that mental energy is finite and its depletion has an adverse effect on self-control.

One of Baumeister's experiments showed people's difficulty in avoiding temptation when faced with choices that defy a solution. For example, one study involved chocolate chip cookies and geometry problems. It required some participants to draw upon their willpower when offered chocolate chip cookies. Researchers then found that they gave up earlier when working on geometry problems than other participants, who could eat the cookies if they wanted to do so. Baumeister concluded that willpower is a form of mental energy that, if overused, could, like a muscle, become fatigued.

Parole Decisions

Researchers have frequently studied how judges decide on paroling prisoners. The studies show how decision fatigue affects these judges. In fact, researchers examined over 1,100 cases over the course of a year, and they consistently found that a prisoner's chances of being given parole rested on one important element, all things being equal: the time the court scheduled their parole hearing.

"Prisoners who had earlier scheduled appointments received parole in around 70 percent of cases, whereas prisoners with later parole hearings were granted parole around 10 percent fewer cases"

— (TIERNEY, J., 2011)

It was simply the mental work required in deciding on parole that induced the judges to use the default option always available: deny parole. The later in the day it became, the more decision fatigue affected the outcome of the hearing.

How to Avoid Decision Fatigue

One way to avoid decision fatigue is to not make so many decisions, as Barack Obama and Mark Zuckerberg have done by wearing essentially the same outfit every day, and as Steve Jobs did with his signature black jeans, jacket, and t-shirt.

Another way to accomplish this is by creating and sticking to daily or weekly routines: strict bedtimes and wake-ups and specific days allotted for exercise or chores.

Because optimal blood glucose levels are another factor that contributes to consistent decision-making, it might be best to snack on nutritious items throughout the day or to defer important decisions until after one has eaten.

Getting enough rest and relaxation also helps with better decision-making. A good night's sleep, breaks throughout the day, and vacations are all important for a person to maintain an optimal cognitive load, as Freud would put it.

SUNK COST FALLACY

When people fall victim to the sunk cost fallacy, they are making decisions that are so highly influenced by their emotions that the decisions are irrational. The sunk cost fallacy means, as its name suggests, that irrecoverable assets have been expended on a project that somewhere along the way turns out not to be beneficial to the investor. Although the fallacy is often commonly used to describe financial decisions, it applies to just about any undertaking where the time and effort already expended do not rationally justify spending any more time, effort, or money. The person is best advised to "cut their losses," but they soldier on, regardless.

The sunk cost fallacy is identifiable in an individual's small, day-to-day decisions and also looms in decisions made by governments and giant companies. When a person makes such a decision, one could say their ego has taken control and dominated their rational mind. Governments and large companies make these decisions for more complex reasons, but, like a person's ego, they too are bowing at the court of public opinion.

The idea of the sunk cost fallacy came about because of the efforts of economists and behavioral scientists to understand humanity's penchant for making irrational decisions that go against participants' best interests.

The first proponent of the idea, famed behavioral scientist Richard Thaler, theorized that when people pay more for goods or services, they are more likely to use them (Thaler, R. 1980, p. 47). A few years after Thaler published his theory, two psychologists, Hal Arkes and Catherine Blumer, conducted several experiments to prove it, which they rephrased as "a greater tendency to continue an endeavor once an investment in money, effort, or time has been made" (1985, p. 124).

In one study, the pair studied participants who they asked to imagine they had paid for two ski trips: one to Michigan and the other to Wisconsin. The Michigan trip at $100 was twice as expensive as the $50 Wisconsin trip. They were told that the Wisconsin trip would be more enjoyable; unfortunately, the trips were on the same weekend. Fifty-four percent of the participants chose the Michigan trip, although the more rational decision would have been to go on the Wisconsin trip, which would have been more enjoyable. They lost the costs of both trips either way. The psychologists decided the sunk cost fallacy played a role in the decisions made by over half the participants, because the greater investment was for the Michigan trip.

Younger People Are More Prone to the Fallacy

When people continue watching a movie which they find boring after 30 minutes, they are experiencing the sunk cost fallacy. They continue to watch because they have already invested 30 minutes of their time on it.

Psychologist JoNell Strough, who with her team of researchers were investigating how age affects decision-making, chose two groups of people to take part in her study: some 18-27 years old and some

58-91 years old. The team found that the younger a participant was, the more likely it was that they would continue watching a boring movie.

All participants saw two vignettes. In the first, they were told they spent almost eleven dollars on a pay-for-TV film, but that they had become bored after five minutes. In the second, they were told they had been watching a boring movie and had again become bored after five minutes. However, the second time they watched the movie for free. They had to choose options for each scenario, quit watching, give the movie five more minutes, watch ten more minutes, watch thirty more minutes, or watch until the movie ended.

The older participants mainly avoided the sunk cost fallacy and did not watch the movie for very long. They also stayed consistent with this behavior through both scenarios. Younger people were more influenced by the sunk cost fallacy and proved less consistent in their decisions (Strough, J., Mehta, C. M., McFall, J. P., & Schuller, K. L., 2008).

The Concorde Fallacy

The so-called "Concorde Fallacy" exemplifies the way the sunk cost fallacy can affect decisions on a large scale. The French and British governments and these countries' engine manufacturers financed the project of building huge, supersonic commercial passenger jets. Initial cost estimates came in close to $100 million. However, as the project progressed, it became clear to all concerned that the planes would never recoup the costs of building them (Arkes, H. R., & Ayton, P., 1999).

The program exhibited huge cost overruns, in the billions of pounds, far above the original estimate, so they made very few Concorde jets, just fourteen. Both governments and the manufacturers continued with the project, and the jets flew from 1975 to 2003, when one crashed, killing all aboard. Altogether, the project had cost 3.4 billion pounds (4.7 billion U.S. dollars), and Airbus and British Airways bought the planes at a huge discount, because the British and French governments absorbed much of this cost. These entities followed through because they had already invested so much money and time on the project.

How to Avoid the Sunk Cost Fallacy

In order to avoid the sunk cost fallacy, a person must focus their attention on the present and the future rather than stewing over past commitments. What are the costs and benefits now? What will they be a few months or years from now? Those are the questions on which a person must concentrate.

When adopting this attitude, a person must often ignore their deep emotional involvement over what has occurred. A person who falls victim to the fallacy also might be trying to follow the "don't waste" rule for entrepreneurs attempting to start a new company. As in, "don't waste your money." But they are carrying this idea to unacceptable extremes.

RECIPROCATION TENDENCY

An unwatched reciprocation tendency may subtly cause mindless behavior, with many extreme or dangerous consequences.

— FARNAM STREET BLOG

Reciprocal behavior represents both the best and the worst aspects of human nature. It can cause extreme violence but also kind behavior. It is responsible for the cruel acts of war, invasion, and feuds, as well as for the establishment of stable relationships based mainly on trust and love, with a bit of reciprocity thrown into the mix.

Reciprocity is so helpful to cultural development that it has become a behavior ingrained in the human subconscious. Famed paleoanthropologist Richard Leakey in his book *Origins Reconsidered*, which he wrote in collaboration with science writer Roger Lewin, believed that a sharing economy among early humans goes back much further than 45,000 years ago when *homo sapiens* came on the scene. In fact, *homo erectus*, whose origins can be traced to two million years ago, already had differentiated themselves from apes by sharing their food:

The sharing of food among members of hunter-gatherer bands is more than an economic transaction. It is the focus of complex social interaction, alliance formation, and ritual... Also important in the collective life of early foraging people was an intensification of what Glynn called 'social chess,' a deep understanding and manipulation of other individuals' motivations and needs, social *reciprocity* (my ital.) (1992, p. 181).

Reciprocities create interdependencies that bind people into groups, whether it be family, industry, or an entire country. These interdependencies combine to make life easier for everyone involved; consider, for example, children's schooling, housing, transportation, or jobs. It is what makes lending even possible, or providing aid when people need it. It is central to family life at any stage.

Negative Reciprocation

Reciprocity has its dark side, as hate engenders more hate. Unless countered with a sense of moral responsibility, a negative downward spiral can cause rampant, mindless destruction. Take, for example, the Iraq War. The lie perpetuated by the American side led to the deaths of many thousands of troops and civilians and culminated in an Islamic cult, or so-called caliphate, dedicated to the West's destruction. And of course history provides many more extreme examples: World War II, the crusades, the depredations of Genghis Khan, etc.

Hammurabi (1792-1750 BCE) enshrined laws entailing reciprocity for evil deeds into his Code, which lists crimes and their respective punishments for the ancient Babylonians. It is not the first code of laws in Mesopotamia, but it is the most inclusive; until the Byzantine emperor Justinian I (482-565 AD) no one wrote any better ones (Wikipedia). The basic principle behind these laws was literally an eye for an eye, but punishment for the criminal varied depending on the status of the victim. If a citizen injured a freeman or slave, they could get away with a fine and did not suffer the same injury as their victims (Wikipedia).

Uninvited Favors

The reciprocity tendency is so powerful that people feel an obligation to people who give them favors even if they did not want the favor and actually dislike whatever they got or the person who bestowed the favor.

A keen observer of the impact of influence on marketing, Robert Cialdini (2021) has arrived at a rule that

---

"the person who acts in a certain way toward us is entitled to a similar return action."

— ROBERT CIALDINI (2021)

He researched this idea after an experience with a Boy Scout who wanted to sell him $5 tickets to the Scouts Circus. When Cialdini passed on the tickets, the boy offered to sell him chocolate bars for a dollar each. Cialdini bought two and then realized the reciprocity tendency was in effect because, "(a) I do not like chocolate bars; (b) I do like dollars; (c) I was standing there with two of his chocolate bars; and (d) he was walking away with two of my dollars."

Cialdini arrived at the following conclusion:

"the person who acts in a certain way toward us is entitled to a similar return action."

— CIALDINI

So if someone offers to give you a pen or even just a cup of coffee, it is more than likely they are expecting something in return. This is behind the free address labels or greeting cards that charities mail out. They would not be doing it unless the strategy was effective.

The Reciprocity Tendency in Wage Disparities

Fehr and Gächter (2000) showed that the reciprocity tendency affects many economic decisions, especially contracts.

The unfairness of wage distribution is a case in point. It can happen that a company's CEO does the board of directors a favor by increasing the compensation of each individual board member. The board raises the CEO's salary. This can repeat itself indefinitely. The process becomes totally unfair when the company hires compensation consultants to ensure that no other employees get similar wage increases.

The Reciprocity Tendency and the Watergate Affair

A misadventure that resulted in the resignation of a United States president may not have occurred if it were not for the reciprocity tendency. The idea to break into Democratic headquarters at the Watergate Hotel in Washington, D.C., was the brainchild of G. Gordon Liddy, one of President Richard M. Nixon's staffers with a dubious reputation.

However, widely unknown are the discussions that preceded the break-in, Liddy had grander ideas than just pilfering the records of their rivals. He had, in fact, three plans: one costing $1 million, a second costing around $500,000, and the Watergate burglary, which Liddy described as a "mere" quarter of the originally proposed price.

Liddy's original plan was outrageous. He wanted a "chase plane," a kidnapping, a yacht with high-class call girls, and a mugging squad. When he honed this all down to a mere break-in, his superiors went along, possibly with a sense of relief. This was the dangerous effect of the reciprocity tendency taken to extremes (Farnam Street Blog).

How to Avoid It

The reciprocity tendency resides in the subconscious, so probably we cannot tame it in many scenarios. In fact, one may not wish to avoid its benign effects. With big decisions, whether they involve important purchases or punching someone in the face, the best plan is to have an agreement with yourself to wait it out and make a more rational decision a day later.

13

DUNNING KRUGER EFFECT

Those most lacking in knowledge and skills are least able to appreciate that lack.

— WILLIAM POUNDSTONE (2016)

In April 1995, a short but very rotund man robbed two Pittsburgh banks while unmasked and waving a gun. Because of his size, the man was impossible to miss and, in addition, security cameras captured his face, which was soon broadcast on the local news. Shortly thereafter, police showed up at his apartment and arrested him.

"But I wore the juice!" he explained on his way downtown for questioning. It turned out that the man, McArthur Wheeler, had heard that lemon juice can be used as invisible ink. With that in mind, he had painted his face with the juice. His eyes became so inflamed he could hardly see. Still, he went ahead with his plans, confident that the lemon juice would make his face invisible to any security cameras.

Besides going into the annals of the world's dumbest criminals, Wheeler captured the attention of David Dunning, a Cornell psychology professor, and caused the worthy professor to study a problem he may have often encountered in the classroom: incompetent people are incapable of knowing that they are incompetent. Together with one of his grad students, Justin Kruger, they explored this idea in four studies that assessed participants' abilities in domains where wisdom, knowledge, or "savvy" were crucial: humor, logical reasoning (two studies), and English grammar.

Their 1999 paper, "Unskilled and Unaware of It: How Difficulties in Recognizing One's Own Incompetence Lead to Inflated Self-Assessments," inspired satirists and musicians. They won an Ig Nobel prize in 2000. In 2017, Marc Abrams wrote the lyrics to

The Incompetence Opera, complete with the "Dunning Kruger Song," sung to music by Puccini (Improbable Research, 2021). People widely shared a YouTube video featuring actor John Cleese. Cleece explained the Dunning-Kruger effect this way:

"If you're very, very stupid, how can you possibly realize that you're very, very stupid? You'd have to be relatively intelligent to realize how stupid you are....And this explains not just Hollywood but almost the entirety of Fox News"

— JOHN CLEESE (POUNDSTONE)

Of course, being conscious of the Dunning-Kruger effect is not a recent phenomenon. The great Chinese sage Confucius (551-479 BCE) said:

"Real knowledge is to know the extent of one's ignorance"

— CONFUCIUS (551-479 BCE)

(MURPHY, M. 2017)

Or as Charles Darwin wrote in his book *The Descent of Man,*

"Ignorance more frequently begets confidence than does knowledge"

— CHARLES DARWIN (*THE DESCENT OF MAN*) (CHERRY, K., 2021)

Not only do ill-informed people not know the extent of their own ignorance; they cannot recognize other people's skill and competence. Instead, they think they are actually more skilled and more competent than anyone else.

The Studies

Humor. Dunning and Kruger's social skills test involving participants' judgements about whether a joke was good was unusual because, although the participants were the usual suspects, college undergrads, their control group was actual professional comics. The researchers came up with a list of 30 jokes and asked the comics to rate them as to how funny they were. Originally, 14 comics took part in the study but they omitted the results of one of them because that person's answers disagreed so much with the others.

The researchers focused on humor because being a competent humorist "requires sophisticated knowledge and wisdom about the tastes and reactions of other people" (Dunning and Kruger, 1999, p. 1133). As expected, the participants who scored the lowest when compared to how the comics rated the jokes felt they were better-than-average humorists. In fact, they had overestimated their percentile standings by 46 percent when the researchers averaged all the scores.

Logical Reasoning. After completing the logical reasoning test, which had questions taken from the Law School Admissions Test, participants had to estimate their ability and performance in three different ways. The first two estimates were how they thought they ranked compared to their peers in their psychology course in reasoning ability and regarding their performance on the specific test. Last, they had to estimate how many of the questions they got right.

In analyzing the results, Dunning and Kruger divided the results into quartiles, so that the students who did poorly on the test were in the lower quartile and those who did best were in the upper quartile. On average, the students in the lower quartile estimated their logical reasoning ability to be much higher than shown by their actual scores.

"Although these individuals scored at the 12th percentile on average, they believed that their general logical reasoning ability fell at the 68th percentile and their score on the test fell at the 62nd percentile"

— (DUNNING AND KRUGER, 1999, P. 1125)

The participants in the bottom fourth also overestimated the number of questions they had answered correctly, by 50 percent.

The results from the grammar test showed the same trends as the first two studies.

In the fourth study, Dunning and Kruger wanted to see if the incompetent students could recognize competence in others. They invited the students from the top and lower quartiles back and asked them to grade tests completed by other students. The purpose of this study was to evaluate Dunning and Kruger's third prediction, that incompetent individuals cannot gain any insight into their own incompetence by observing others' behavior.

Each participant had to grade five tests completed by their peers and show the number of questions they thought each of the five had answered correctly. After that, the researchers gave participants their own papers to re-rate their ability relative to their peers.

As expected, participants in the bottom quartile had trouble gauging the competence of other students. Furthermore, they again overestimated their own ability.

As for the students in the top quartile, after they had graded the papers, their estimates of their own ability improved. These results supported the observation that knowledgeable people often underestimate their own ability because they are more aware of what they *don't* know. Then, after they saw how others had fared, they came to realize their own talent.

In later studies, Dunning and his colleagues tested people's knowledge of terms used in various subjects like politics, biology, physics and geography. Those ignorant of these fields often interjected completely made-up terms and then claimed they had some knowledge of the made-up terms.

Consistent with other findings related to the Dunning-Kruger effect, when participants claimed familiarity with a topic, they also claimed they were familiar with the meaningless terms. As Dunning has suggested, the very trouble with ignorance is that it can feel just like expertise (Cherry, K., 2021).

Blind Spots in Cognitive Ability

The ability to consider objectively one's own behavior and abilities, as though from the outside looking in, is metacognition. If a person can only see themselves from a subjective point of view, to themselves they seem as if they are highly skilled, knowledgeable, and superior to others.

Also, when a person has only a limited knowledge of a subject, and they cannot view themselves objectively, to them it can seem they are indeed knowledgeable about that subject.

They may have been using the mental shortcuts, or heuristics, as described in this book. They feel the need to make sense of the complexity all around them and may see patterns when none exist because that is what the human brain demands. Subconsciously, their very survival is on the line.

Who Is Affected by this Effect?

Contrary to beliefs expressed by the satirists who have made hay with this topic, whether a person displays the Dunning-Kruger effect has little to do with their IQ. In fact, the Dunning-Kruger effect can apply to just about anyone because the expert in one field can be totally ignorant of another and, contrary to a belief they may hold, their expertise does not carry over into realms totally unfamiliar to them.

In contrast, experts may realize they are well-versed in their field, but tests conducted by Dunning and Kruger showed that high-scoring participants underestimated their own abilities. Their knowledge and expertise also revealed to them how much they did *not* know, in a kind of reverse Dunning-Kruger effect.

14

THE BEN FRANKLIN EFFECT

The Benjamin Franklin Effect is the result of your concept of self coming under attack.

— DAVID MCRANEY (2011)

Polymath Benjamin Franklin was an American Founding Father who accomplished so much in his lifetime, as a printer, newspaper publisher, library and hospital founder, writer, and ambassador, that today he stands on a pedestal, revered by all. But once he was a struggling politician running for the second time for clerk of the general assembly in Philadelphia. Although he won the race, Franklin believed his political future was in doubt because of the animosity of a fellow legislator who gave a long and derogatory speech about him to the entire assembly.

Of course, Franklin was furious, but instead of attacking the man outright with a speech of his own, he considered long and hard what the best course of action would be. He recounts in his autobiography:

Having heard that he had in his library a certain very scarce and curious book, I wrote a note to him, expressing my desire of perusing that book, and requesting he would do me the favour of lending it to me for a few days. He sent it immediately, and I return'd it in about a week with another note, expressing strongly my sense of the favour. When we next met in the House, he spoke to me (which he had never done before), and with great civility; and he ever after manifested a readiness to serve me on all occasions, so that we became great friends, and our friendship continued to his death.

This conscious manipulation of the situation on Franklin's part reveals the vast extent of his social awareness and dexterity. Born into a working class family of 17 children, no one would have believed that he could have come this far and accomplished so much. He had such an innate knowledge of human psychology that he could initiate an action that academics today run experiments to explain. Why would doing a favor for someone who dislikes you or feels neutral about you change that person's opinion of you? People have written complicated studies and lengthy books about this topic.

The general answer to this quandary is reference to another cognitive bias, cognitive dissonance, which I will discuss in more detail in the next chapter. Doing a favor for someone you dislike or perhaps have no feelings about puts a person in a state of confusion. This is all going on subconsciously, but MRI scans tell quite a story. If a person sees statements opposing their own beliefs, the highest portions of the cortex in charge of rational thought start getting less blood. The brain cannot take the contradictions presented to it and actually starts shutting down until the person sees statements confirming their own beliefs. To try it at home without the benefit of an MRI, simply watch politicians or pundits speak who have views antithetical to your own for fifteen minutes. This will prove intensely painful (McRaney, D., 2011).

In response to their confused state of mind, the person who did the favor questions their own opinion about the person who asked for the favor. Their rationale goes something like this: "I did so-and-so a favor and agreed to their request. Therefore, I must like them. You only do favors for people you like, right?" So old opinions about the person requesting the favor go by the wayside and positive thoughts and opinions about this person replaced them. Franklin could make a dangerous political rival into a lifelong friend simply by requesting the loan of a book. Of course, the fact that Franklin had founded the first subscription library in America helped matters along. That such an erudite, famous, and wealthy man appreciated the rival's taste in books flattered him.

Besides cognitive dissonance, the self-perception theory can also explain some cases of the Benjamin Franklin effect. According to this theory, when people lack any kind of concrete attitude towards another person or a situation, they may regard themselves and scrutinize their own actions to explain their behavior to themselves. From their own actions, they deduce what their attitude actually is. So when people perform a favor for another about whom they have no opinion because they do not know the person very well, if at all, they see that they have performed this kindness and conclude they must like the person (Effectiviology).

Sometimes, it does not have to be a cognitive bias that causes a person to like someone who asks a favor of them. Maybe they simply feel acknowledged and respected, and that can cause them to like the requestor.

The Benjamin Franklin Effect in Daily Life

Even a minor favor can turn the tables, especially if you ask a person for a favor who you know dislikes you. When people feel neutral about doing the favor and blow it off as perhaps the cost of doing business or they think they will derive some benefit from the favor in the future, the Benjamin Franklin effect may not take place at all.

Although people are more likely to experience this effect when they have negative or neutral attitudes about the person they are helping, the effect can come into play, even if they actually like the person a bit. This is particularly true if the favor is quite a large one.

Taking advantage of the Benjamin Franklin effect may help you gain more friends, especially if you believe they will like you more if they think you will reciprocate. It is important to note that the favor requested can be quite a small one. What is important is that you asked them.

Some people are afraid to ask for help because they do not think there is a likelihood people will help them. What they do not realize is that there is a social cost of refusing to grant a favor, simply because the urge to cooperate is in our genes. People want to avoid saying no. Also, another bias, the illusion of transparency, comes into play as well. People think others see through them to their motivations when usually such is not the case. The person of whom you are asking the favor probably does not realize you are simply trying to build rapport.

When people try to use the Benjamin Franklin effect on you, it is helpful to recognize the technique. Sometimes it is harmless; the other person is simply trying to build rapport. However, salespeople may try to use it to their advantage in order to sell you something you do not want later on.

The Negative Benjamin Franklin Effect

The negative Benjamin Franklin effect can cause aggressive people to increase how much they dislike a person after they have treated that person badly. They do this because they may need to justify their negative actions to themselves or

---

"because they might base their attitude toward that person on their own negative actions"

— (EFFECTIVIOLOGY)

This effect may help explain atrocities that become worse over time, the more the assailants convince themselves that their punitive actions are justified.

15

COGNITIVE DISSONANCE

Since the 1950s, researchers have studied cognitive dissonance. Into this concept fit several cognitive biases, including the Benjamin Franklin effect, discussed in the last chapter, the sunk cost fallacy, discussed in Chapter 11, hindsight bias (Chapter 5), and confirmation bias (Chapter 2). It describes feelings of stress, stress a person can experience when confronted with a belief or theory or fact opposing their own belief, theory, or understanding of a fact. The stress can be small, simply a feeling of discomfort, or it might lead to major disorders like depression and anxiety. We can connect the difference in reactions to how deeply a person feels about their original belief. For example, a confirmed animal lover who is a vegan may feel more stress if they eat meat than a person who talks all the time about exercise but stays on their couch.

When faced with this kind of stress, a person can make a few different choices. Maybe they will keep their belief secret if they know those around them hold the opposite opinion. They may black out any kind of information opposing their belief. It is possible they may continuously rationalize their opposing beliefs or minimize their importance. Or they might change their beliefs to fit the additional facts presented to them. However, per our discussion of the confirmation bias, many find it extremely difficult to do the latter. Here, cognitive dissonance becomes a learning tool that prompts people to confront their actions and attitudes.

Sometimes, a person may not be aware that they are holding opposing beliefs. In that case, they would not feel the effects of cognitive dissonance. Also, the degree they felt the dissonance can differ from person to person, as certain people can better tolerate uncertainty and inconsistency.

Attitude vs. Behavior

Experiments in social psychology have shown that people's behavior often creates their attitudes and beliefs and not the other way around, as one might logically assume. It is a way of putting the cart before the horse, and it happens time after time.

The psychologist who invented the concept of cognitive dissonance, Leon Festinger, noted this apparent contradiction in one of his studies in the 1950s. He and his collaborator, James Carlsmith, came up with an extremely boring task, such as turning pegs in a pegboard for an hour. The participants then got either only a dollar or twenty dollars, but they had to tell other participants waiting to take the test that the tasks were interesting and fun. Later, the participants had to evaluate the experiment, and the ones who got only a dollar then rated the tasks more fun than the ones paid $20.

Festinger and Carlsmith concluded the difference in their ratings was because of cognitive dissonance. Being paid $20 seemed like a just reimbursement for the uninteresting job, so those participants experienced no cognitive dissonance. However, being paid only $1 does not work as an incentive for lying. To resolve this dissonance, those participants convinced themselves that the task had been fun, just as they had said.

For more examples on how this might work, ask yourself these questions: Do you put on a suit to go to work because you desire to act professionally? Or do you act professionally *because* you donned the suit? Are you a champion of social programs and thus decide the Democratic ticket fits your needs, or do you champion social programs because you vote Democrat? There is research saying it is the latter in both cases.

The Aliens Are Coming! The Aliens Are Coming!

In 1954, Festinger conceived his cognitive dissonance theory after a bit of real life research into a Chicago doomsday cult whose leader, Dorothy Martin, convinced her followers that a huge flood on December 21, 1954, would sweep away the world as they knew it. Festinger and his colleagues infiltrated the cult and got to know some of its members. Although those on the fringes of the cult did little to save themselves, considering the prophecy, true believers sold their houses and gave away everything they owned to be ready for their saviors, as Dorothy Martin had also prophesied that an alien spacecraft would such them up and take them to safety.

Festinger was quite eager to know what would happen when the 21st arrived and there was no flood and no alien spacecraft. His hypothesis was that the members would face a choice: see themselves as naïve ignorant bumpkins or assume that their faith had spared both themselves and the rest of the world. It was the latter option the members chose. Rather than taking a gigantic blow to their self-esteem, they contacted the media and said they had splendid news; all that positive energy they had exuded had touched God so much that He saved the Earth from annihilation.

Later, Festinger wrote this about the experience:

Suppose an individual believes something with his whole heart; suppose further that he has a commitment to this belief, that he has taken irrevocable actions because of it; finally, suppose that he is presented with evidence, unequivocal and undeniable evidence, that his belief is wrong: What will happen?

The individual will frequently emerge, not only unshaken, but even more convinced of the truth of his beliefs than ever before. Indeed, he may even show a new fervor about convincing and converting other people to his view (Festinger,L., Riecken, R. and Schachter, S. (2019) *When Prophecy Fails, 1956).*

3 Ways to Resolve Cognitive Dissonance

Three methods to reduce cognitive dissonance include: 1) Change the belief(s), attitude(s) and/or behavior(s) so they do not clash. This can be difficult. For example, giving up smoking is so difficult, even though the smoker is aware of the negative effects, because smoking is both a learned behavior and an addiction. 2) Take in new information that outweighs one of the dissonant beliefs. However, a person might find research that supports both sides. For example, the smoker is aware of research that shows the negative effects of smoking. However, they might also have come across research that says that the research has not completely proved that there will be negative effects. 3) Convince yourself that the new information is not that important, anyway. A smoker could say they prefer a short life where they can smoke to a longer life where they can't in a "live for today" attitude (McCloud, S., 2018).

16

DECOY EFFECT

The decoy effect is a sales strategy that can cause a person buying more than they actually want or need. It occurs when a person does not have an either-or choice but must choose among three alternatives. The third choice, or the decoy, is inferior to the other two, but asymmetrically. It is completely inferior to one option, which is the target the sales people want the customer to buy, but only partially inferior to the other (the competition).

The decoy effect, or the "asymmetric dominance effect," may be familiar to anyone visiting a movie theater who decides they want some popcorn. There is a small bag that costs the least—say around $3.00. Then there is the medium-sized bucket of popcorn (the decoy) that costs, say, $6.50. And then there is the giant bucket of popcorn (the target) costing $7.00. The customer does not want that much popcorn, but the small bag is so puny and the difference between the medium and large buckets of popcorn is only .50. So they waste their money and maybe waste their food by buying the giant bucket. They would have been satisfied with the medium bucket for a fair price (say $5) but by making the medium bucket the decoy, the theater owners are raking in the dough at the concessions stand.

When faced with a choice like the one above, consumers often go with the most expensive option because it seems like the best deal, even though it is not what they want or need. Long term, the decoy effect in sales can have a big negative impact on a person's finances.

How It Works

To recapitulate, the target is what someone else, like a business, wants you to choose. They then set out a competitor to the target and, finally, a decoy, to encourage a person to get the target. Both the target and the competitor dominate the decoy by at least two factors asymmetrically so that it is better on both counts, but the competitor can be worse on one count but better on the second.

In the popcorn example, the customer evaluates their options based on size and price. The medium popcorn is the decoy because the other two dominate it asymmetrically. It is bigger than the small bag of popcorn but more expensive. So, it is only partially better. The large bucket of popcorn is superior on both counts, as it is larger and only costs a little more. In one experiment, people chose the large popcorn if the only other choice was the small, but even more people bought the large popcorn when the researchers added the decoy, the medium popcorn, making the choice of the large "irresistible" (The Decision Lab).

The decoy effect works on peoples' subconscious to nudge them to behave in a certain manner. Decoys affect people without them realizing it. It is what we call a "behavioral nudge" that steers people in a certain direction without technically violating their free will. It works because people are not all that aware of why they act a certain way and not another. A person can believe that they are deliberate about their choices when actually they are not cognizant of all the factors influencing those choices.

Decoys Facilitate Decision-Making

With a decoy in the mix of choices available to them, a person can more easily justify their choice. They can point to the decoy as the reason they have made that choice. They thus make the process less stressful than it would otherwise have been. The idea of preference uncertainty is relevant here because, in order to be more certain about what they actually want, people prefer a small range of factors on which they can focus in order to decide. The decoy effect capitalizes on this quality by manipulating the number of choices in a set of options. Usually, if they provide over four options, the decoy effect will no longer work. Instead, the customer will become overwhelmed and unable to make a choice at all.

An Excuse to Spend More Money

Including a decoy in a scenario where at first there were only two options can help people find it easier to decide. When they have a plethora of options, they actually find it harder to decide because so many choices make the process confusing. When they have only two options, they have to decide which one is better based on over two factors: perhaps price, speed, and battery life. An expensive phone may be speedier but have a short battery life, while a cheaper phone may have a better battery life but is not as speedy.

When marketers introduce a third phone that is far more expensive but has an even shorter battery life than the first two, the consumer stops considering the price and only decides based on two factors: the speed and the battery life. They then ignore the least expensive version to go with the medium-priced version, which is just as speedy as the most expensive phone *and* has a better battery life.

Introducing the decoy phone has provided the person with the excuse they need to go with the more expensive model, even though it costs more than they originally budgeted for.

Dealing with Loss Aversion

As covered in Chapter 4, people are much more distressed by loss than happy about gain. In fact, they are about twice as likely to grieve a loss than to feel excited about a gain. The question remains, loss compared to what? What is a factor against which people measure their losses?

When confronted by three choices wherein one choice is a decoy, the decoy can serve as a reference point from which to compare advantages and disadvantages. The seller can move the decoy around, thus moving the reference point by which the buyer evaluates gains vs. losses.

Another way decoys play upon loss aversion is that when faced with three choices, buyers tend to gravitate toward a higher price (the target) if there is a big difference in quality among the items.

The Trap of Rationality

More than likely, awareness that the decoy effect exists does not help a person avoid it. It is a bias that works very well because it just feels rational. When a person goes to the trouble of carefully examining their choice, they may find instead that they are coming up with more justifications for having made the choice. Studies have shown that

---

"thoughtful introspection does not correlate with rational decisions or correct outcomes"

— (HENDRICKS. K., 2016)

It is important to be accurate. It is important to be speedy. The brain cannot do both at the same time. The reason that the decoy effect is so prevalent and so effective is because the human brain has evolved to make a "good enough" decision in the least amount of time.

Scientists have shown that the decoy effect helps people be calmer when deciding. MRI scans show that the part of the brain controlling fear and other negative emotions, the amygdala, becomes less active when researchers added a decoy during a study where people had to decide on more than one option. Actually, the scans showed less activity in the brain in all areas concerned with decision making, like the part that processes numerical magnitude or the way it handles self evaluation of preferences. The brain released more dopamine, a calming substance (Hendricks. K., 2016).

Here are three ways to counter the decoy effect. First, be aware of the human penchant for rationalizing poor decisions. Second, keep an eye out for items for sale in sets of three. Third, be sure to calculate costs per unit. How much does every inch added to a tv screen cost? The price of food per ounce? Asymmetric relationships among purchases may mean there is a decoy in the mix. After calculating these costs, fourth, calculate how much you will buy within a certain time period.

17

THE SPOTLIGHT EFFECT

The spotlight effect describes how people believe others see them when they think their appearance and actions loom large in others' perception of them. The fact is, most people concentrate on their own concerns and do not notice things like a small stain on someone's clothing, or that their handbag is fake Kate Spade, or the negative comment they made in a group discussion, or mistakes they made during a sporting event. Conversely, others also do not recall a lot of a person's positive attributes, such as the purse is a real Kate Spade handbag, they contributed positively to a group discussion in a way they themselves thought was memorable, their clothing is immaculate, and they completed a challenge like participating in a real game or a video game with no errors.

For example, when participants in a study dressed in a T-shirt they thought was embarrassing walked in on a group of people filling out questionnaires, the researchers later asked both groups about their impressions of the T-shirts. It turned out that the group who wore the T-shirts wildly exaggerated the reactions of the others, who were filling out the questionnaires. The experimenters measured the spotlight effect by the difference between the estimates by the person wearing the T-shirt and the group filling out the questionnaire.

The T-shirt in question depicted Barry Manilow, whose music the researchers believed at the time was not popular among college undergraduates (the experiment took place at Cornell University in 2000). The researchers asked the people recruited to observe the T-shirt wearer if they recognized the person depicted on the shirt when the target came into the room and sat down briefly among the group.

The difference between the target's estimate of how many recognized Barry Manilow as opposed to how many actually did so was close to fifty percent. The target wearing the shirt thought that half the group recognized the musician on their shirt when only a quarter of the group did. They ran the experiment several times, and the mean discrepancy turned out to be forty percent. These researchers also introduced a delay condition in their research in which the target with the Barry Manilow T-shirt stayed in the group for longer. Under these conditions, the target was less likely to overestimate reactions to the shirt because they had become accustomed to wearing it. The researchers concluded:

People typically understand that their own actions and appearance are not as salient to others as they are to themselves, and they take that into account when estimating how others perceive them. But because such adjustments are insufficient, they typically end up overestimating their own prominence in the eyes of others (Gilovich, T., Savistsky, K., and Medvee, V., 2000).

The researchers also proposed that something like a reverse spotlight effect might apply when people are not conscious of their own behavior or appearance, yet their actions are very noticeable to others.

Why It Happens

The spotlight effect occurs because of the cumulative effect of other subconscious cognitive biases that block an individual from determining exactly what their impact on others is.Two of the most common of these are the anchoring bias (Chapter 6) and the egocentric bias (Chapter 7).

The egocentric bias has to do with the difficulty people have in understanding others' perspectives. The spotlight effect studies focus on people's assessments of how much they are the focus of others' attention. What is difficult for people to do is to escape the anchor of their own experience when trying to estimate how their actions appear to others.

Another bias that comes into play here is naïve realism (Chapter 25), which is when a person assumes that their perception of reality is actually the correct one. They believe they are being objective when observing reality and cannot recognize the subjective nature of their assessments. Because people believe in the absolute truth of their own perceptions, they think others will see everything the same way they do.

The self-as-target bias magnifies the spotlight effect. This is when people believe something disproportionately targeted all actions and or events at them. This bias represents people's confusion between what is available to them vs. what is available to others (Gilovich, T., Savistsky, K., and Medvee, V., 2000).

The Spotlight Effect and Social Anxiety

Everyone experiences the spotlight effect, because no one can completely escape the bounds of self and their ego's defences against attacks on their self worth. We thus cannot downplay its importance. The need to belong, to not be ostracized, is bred into the human race. As primates living in harsh conditions, our ancestors knew that to become isolated meant certain death. Thus, the brain perceives the opinion of the group and the need to be accepted by the group as matters of life and death.

Social anxiety is a condition that is far from normal nervousness. Researchers link it to actual differences in brain activity and brain chemistry. A person who suffers from social anxiety may realize that their feelings are irrational but they cannot change them (Cuncic, A., 2021).

When people suffer from social anxiety, the spotlight effect can have very negative consequences because of the way this combination affects a person's interactions with others. What this means is that they experience serious blocks to their prospects, career, and the life they want to live.

People with social anxiety should focus their attention outward and notice other people's reactions to them. That way, the person leaves off paying so much attention to how anxious they feel and instead notices the way people are actually paying attention to them.

Another related bias is the illusion of transparency, wherein people believe others know what they are actually thinking. This illusion can also feel magnified in people with social anxiety, but it is more relevant to the spotlight effect (Cuncic, A., 2021).

18

THE IKEA EFFECT

The phrase "a labor of love" holds more meaning than one could have thought possible for an over-worn cliche because it holds so true in the Ikea effect. The Ikea effect is a strange phenomenon whereby when people buy something and then must contribute to its assembly, they do not subtract the costs of their labor from the cost of the product and instead value the product much more than if they had purchased it ready-made.

Various studies have explained the Ikea effect. We term one "effort justification." This research shows that the more effort people have made in following a pursuit, the more they value it. This is even true for animals, like rats, that were found to prefer sources of food that they were required to make an effort to get.

However, if the people are unsuccessful in their efforts to make something, the Ikea effect goes away. In fact, failure can have adverse consequences because people ruminate on their failure and experience regret that they could not complete the task.

Researchers at two business schools and a university undertook a study about this anomaly, which they dubbed "the Ikea effect," because they wanted to understand the connection between effort and liking, and also because they believed that knowledge about this effect would interest marketers who wish to engage their customers (Norton, M, Mochen, D. and Ariely, D.., 2012).

In their four studies, Norton et al. enlisted consumers to assemble Ikea furniture, build sets of Legos, and fold origami. Their results confirm research done a few years earlier that showed that, for example, asking people to add an egg to a cake mix resulted in them preferring that cake mix over others that did not require adding an egg. A couple of other activities that were studied also confirmed this: Build-a-Bear, in which customers had to make their own stuffed bear, and an offering by farmers called a "haycation," where visitors staying at a farm paid to harvest their own food.

In their first experiment, the researchers avoided any extra value a person might place on a decorative object by having participants value a totally utilitarian object: a plain storage box manufactured by Ikea that required assembly. Some participants had to assemble this box, but other participants were just given the box, totally assembled. After the participants chosen to assemble the box had finished the project, all the participants bid on their box. The people who had assembled their box bid higher than those who had been given the box. The builders also responded that they liked their box better than did the non-builders.

In Love With Their Imperfect Creations

Participants made origami cranes or frogs in another experiment that showed how much a person can love their own particular creation. When they bid on the tiny paper creatures, they bid five times higher than other participants in the study, who only had the job of evaluating these creations before bidding on them. Interestingly, the makers of these humble pieces of art believed that their creations were worth almost as much as origami fashioned by experts.

Norton et al. also investigated how people felt about an object they had built and then had to disassemble. Here, the Ikea effect totally disappears. So making something when it turns out okay, at least in the eyes of its maker, does turn out to be a labor of love.

Cognitive Dissonance

Cognitive dissonance drives the Ikea effect (Chapter 15), which explains that contradictory opinions or beliefs can be very disorienting. A person will try to reduce the discomfort by changing their behavior or altering their beliefs.

There is a type of cognitive dissonance, called "effort justification" that helps in understanding the Ikea effect. People who have done something quite difficult, where they spent a lot of effort, want to believe they had a good reason to work that hard. Thus, they place more value or importance on goals they had to work for vs. goals that came to them easily.

This also becomes a self-esteem issue. People want to think of themselves as rational beings, not some sucker who put "sweat equity" into building a dresser when they could have just purchased a new one. They make a mental adjustment and decide the dresser they made is more valuable than other dressers so they can feel their effort is compatible with the outcome.

Also, as exemplified in an earlier chapter on the Dunning-Kruger effect (Chapter 13), people are often more confident in their own abilities than they may have a right to be, objectively. So, this can be another reason they attach more value to things that they have made as opposed to things they can purchase.

Cost of the Ikea Effect

The Ikea effect can lead to people making costly mistakes. They think they are getting a good deal because they overvalue a product they made themselves. A more careful consideration of the proposed project may help a person evaluate it better. They should consider how long it will take them to put the project together and ask themselves if the low price justifies all the time and effort. They should balance convenience vs. the upfront cost prior to making their decision. It might do well to ask for a second opinion from someone who has no investment in the project.

However, one study found advantages to the Ikea effect, in this case, getting children to eat their vegetables. In this study (Radtke et al., 2019) kids were more likely to eat more vegetables if the parents involved them in cooking family meals.

So, in conclusion, simply ask yourself: is a slight difference in price worth taking up your free time to build something?

19

FUNDAMENTAL ATTRIBUTION ERROR (FALSE ATTRIBUTION BIAS)

The fundamental attribution error occurs when a person believes that another's behavior is because of internal factors, like personality (dispositional attribution), when in actuality their behavior springs from some external source out of their control, such as a family emergency (situational attribution). The converse of this is that people often cut themselves some slack and attribute their own behavior to external factors rather than internal ones.

It is possible this subconscious bias originally worked as a heuristic to help people survive in the wild, where snap decisions about another person's character might have made the difference between life or death. However, these days, when we observe another person's angry expression and jump to the conclusion that they are an angry individual, we often could not be more wrong, as it is possible they look angry because they just got insulted or just got some bad news. Making false attributions can really stand in the way of better relationships, and excusing oneself all the time for poor decisions one has made can undermine a person's reputation.

The reason researchers call the bias the fundamental attribution error is because a person has made a fundamental error in attributing the other's actions to their disposition. Conversely, we might think people act a certain way because of their situation, when in fact it is their disposition that is to blame. However, people make the dispositional attribution error because that is the easier decision. It is usually impossible to know what situations may be behind a person's actions. Did a driver speed past you because they are a poor driver or are drunk? That is the easiest choice to make. There is no way of knowing the driver is speeding to the hospital with a wife who is about to give birth. There is no way we can know that someone just got bad news unless we ask them, and that may prove impossible if we simply see a stranger on a crowded sidewalk storming along with a scowl on their face.

Pro- or Anti-Castro?

In the first study of false attribution bias, published in 1967, participants read essays by students who were told they must write a pro-Castro essay or an anti-Castro essay. The participants already knew the writers had no choice about the topic. Yet, when the participants read the pro-Castro essay, they were significantly more likely to assume that the writers were themselves pro-Castro than the people who read the anti-Castro essays (Effectiviology).

Researchers have advanced several reasons outside of heuristics to explain why people make false attributions and mainly focus on personality rather than the other person's situation. Aside from not really knowing what that situation actually is, we may attribute actions to disposition because we would like to believe in a world that is fair. Thus, we believe that people in unfortunate situations are just getting what they deserve. This can cause people to blame the victim instead of the perpetrator. People blame rape victims because they hope to reassure themselves that they are not susceptible to such a tragedy.

Also, people attribute an effect only to causes that are obvious to them. Thus, they see the other person as the primary reference point, while their situation is background noise. Regarding themselves, people are of course more aware of their own circumstances, so they know that there are situational forces acting upon them that cause them to behave a certain way.

Another reason is that people rarely adjust their view to consider facts they know to be true. This is because they do not take in their initial assumptions about another's character simultaneously with knowledge about the person's situation. Initially a person judges another based on what they have observed about their behavior. Only later do they find out that the other person is in a situation out of their control. In such a case, we need to make a deliberate effort to adjust our inferences regarding the other person. This can happen especially if the person making the mistaken inference is under a lot of stress or pressure at work.

Age and cultural differences may need to be accounted for when considering why people make false attributions. It turns out that American children and Hindu adults and children were more prone to look for possible situational explanations for a person's behavior than were American adults.

The reason may be that the United States is an individualistic culture, whereas India is a collectivist culture (Miller, J. G., 1984). By the time they become adults, Americans have adapted themselves to their culture, although their children view things more holistically.

20

BANDWAGON EFFECT

In the 19th century, parades often featured bandwagons, which were ornate floats with a band playing lively music. Spectators watching as the float passed by could jump aboard to sing, dance, or otherwise enjoy the show. Sometimes there would be a prominent politician on the float encouraging people to come on board. Eventually the phrase "jump on the bandwagon" grew to mean voting for such-and-such a politician because otherwise you will miss out on all the fun.

During the last two centuries, psychologists have co-opted the idea of a "bandwagon effect" to label a cognitive bias that encourages people to go along with the crowd, to adopt behaviors, styles, or attitudes simply because everyone else does. The more people "hop on the bandwagon," the more likely it is that others will come on board.

As a cognitive bias, the bandwagon effect developed in humans to help them think faster in sticky situations. However, this bias can be very detrimental to society and to one's own health. It is subconscious and often influences a person to act even if the herd's values and opinions do not reflect their own values and opinions.

The Anti-Vax Movement

The anti-vax movement has been around for a long time. It developed after the government required vaccinations against childhood diseases for children to attend school. People became suspicious that the vaccinations caused autism. Study after study showed this was not the case, but in certain areas of the country, this became a prevalent opinion that eventually resulted in measles outbreaks in those locations.

Another negative effect concerns trends in voting. When people learn that a certain candidate is winning, they may change how they had planned to vote in order to vote for the winning ticket.

Other banwagon effects might simply be neutral, except that most times people are disregarding the option to think for themselves in their desire to belong to the in group. Some other obvious effects are diet, where everyone seems to be following the latest fad diet; fashion, both in decor and clothing; and music, where almost everyone wants to hear the most popular song (the reason behind the "top ten" on the radio). A more recent example of the bandwagon effect is the "social influencer" phenomenon and the way people migrate to certain social networks and stop using others, like Myspace.

The bandwagon effect reflects an intense desire by most people to fit in. When more and more people engage in a certain activity, the desire to join them is close to irresistible. Not only do people usually have an intense desire to conform, they also want to be right and be part of the winning side. People look to others in their group when trying to determine what is acceptable. If everyone else is doing something, then it seems like this is the correct option. Therefore, when invited to a party, they may call other invitees to ask what they are going to wear. Or, they include the type of dress that is acceptable on the invitation.

Nobody wants to be the odd one out. Going along with the group may be a way to gain the group's acceptance and approval.

Trends Are Fleeting

When things happen because of the bandwagon effect, often the situation is extremely volatile. What is up must come down. People who jump on the bandwagon can jump off just as fast. This is why actors and sports figures who enjoy sudden popularity would be wise to save their windfall. Their public is capricious. Trusting that fame will last can be disheartening and the disappointment may lead to self-destructive tendencies. We may deride politicians who keep their posts for too long as "old school." We may deride people once productive in their career as "dinosaurs."

The Bandwagon Effect in Business

The bandwagon effect holds very special meaning in a business sense, both in positive and in negative ways. For example, the bandwagon effect in consumer affairs can be a valuable labor-saving strategy. Here, a consumer is relying on others' research about a product to decide to buy the product. They have outsourced their research to other parties whom they have discerned as more knowledgeable and also reliable. This is the very reason people buy the magazine, *Consumer Reports*.

But sometimes the research they rely on is not very reliable. Marketers often provide it, so deciding to buy a product this way may not be optimal. This may not be so important for individuals purchasing a product, but when companies buy expensive products for production that they have not properly tested, this approach could harm that company.

Also, people may buy products they neither need nor really want, which is detrimental to their bottom line. The bandwagon effect can cause conspicuous consumption, where consumers are purchasing expensive items just to display their wealth (The Investopedia Team, 2020).

Regarding investors, the bandwagon effect looms large and can be very dangerous. Not only do the same kinds of impediments occur that encourage people to get on the bandwagon (social, psychological, and the cost of information-gathering), but the assets themselves rise in price as people jump on the bandwagon. This can cause a feedback loop, and the prices of assets keep on rising until, one day, they do not and the sector crashes. This occurred during the dotcom bubble of the late 1990s, when dozens of fly-by-night companies that had little going for them besides a techie sounding name attracted millions of dollars that the investors ultimately lost (The Investopedia Team, 2020).

21

FRAMING EFFECT

The framing effect is highly connected to loss aversion or prospect theory (Chapter 4). In fact, the same two Israeli psychologists who came up with the idea of prospect theory also researched what they called the framing effect (Tversky, A. and Kahneman, D., 1981). Loss aversion or prospect theory means that when people evaluate certain prospects, they try to avoid risk, even if another choice offers the chance of greater returns.

The way they relate this to framing theory is that people favor one option over another based on the way it is framed, even though both statements mean essentially the same thing.

Tversky and Kahneman's experiment had participants choose an option for a treatment for 600 people with cancer. The two options were:

1. The likelihood that 400 people would die.
2. The 66 percent probability that everyone would die and a 33 percent likelihood of no one dying.

The researchers then presented these options with both a negative framing and a positive framing, i.e. how many would die vs. how many would live. Only 22 percent chose the option when they framed it negatively, as resulting in 400 people dying, vs. 72 percent choosing the first option, as in 200 people living. The results of the experiment showed that when people have options to choose from, not only does the substance of the information influence them but also the framing thereof (Perera, A., 2021).

They have also studied the framing effect on actual cancer patients. The researcher, U.S. health science professor Annette O'Connor, asked two groups of participants to choose between two cancer treatment options. One group was composed of healthy volunteers, but the other one comprised cancer patients, and they had to choose a toxic cancer treatment or a nontoxic one.

The framing occurred in three forms:

1. probability of living (positive frame).
2. probability of dying (negative frame)
3. probability of living and dying (mixed frame)

If they framed the probabilities negatively, and the probability of living was below 50 percent, participants were less likely to choose the more effective toxic treatment. O'Connor concluded,

---

"a negative frame or probability level below 0.5 would seem to stimulate a "dying mode" type of value system in which quality of life becomes more salient in decision making than quantity of life"

— (O'CONNOR, A. M., 1989)

Framing Effect in Plea Bargaining

Stephanos Bibas, a U.S. law professor and judge, wrote in the *Harvard Law Review* that defendants view a plea bargain through a "loss frame" and thus are often less likely to accept them (Bibas, S., 2004). Bibas was studying the impact of various cognitive biases in legal trials. Defendants view plea bargains as a loss because they are used to being free. Any loss of freedom, as contemplated in a plea bargain, is a loss, even if the plea bargain promises less jail time than would a conviction in court without such a bargain.

However, a defendant in pre-trial detention will often see plea bargains "through the lens of gains." Such a defendant "is more likely to view prison as the baseline and eventual freedom as a gain, particularly if freedom is possible in weeks or months" (Bibas, S., 2004).

Junior Economists vs. Senior Economists

One study attempted to find out how economists revert to the framing effect when making decisions. The experimenters assumed that these experimental economists would know about the framing effect and be resistant to it.

They framed an invitation to attend a conference to the economists regarding registering early vs. later registration. One group got information about registering for the conference early that was framed in a positive way. Their information read that paying less for the conference when registering early was a discount. The second group got the information framed in a negative way: they termed paying more when paying later as a late penalty.

"The results showed that while the junior experimental economists were influenced by the framing effect, the more senior economists were not"

— (PERERA, A., 2021)

How to Avoid the Framing Effect

What are the details in advertisements, usually appearing below the main ad in fine print, whether the ad is online or in print? People not wanting to get caught up in the framing effect should notice these details and rather than the enticing promises. Can you rephrase something so it means the same thing but has a positive connotation if negative or a negative connotation if positive? This is a good practice to engage in prior to deciding.

Research options from a wide variety of sources before deciding on a course of action.

If a political candidate is being demonized by certain media outlets, seek alternative opinions elsewhere, preferably from the candidate's supporters.

In order to avoid the framing effect, you will have to do a little digging and a little research on your own.

22

EXTENSION NEGLECT

Extension neglect has to do with how a person evaluates a study. It is a cognitive bias whereby the person does not consider the number of participants in the study when that is very relevant to the study's conclusions. For example, if one participant scores very high or very low, and the number of participants is too small, this will skew the results to such a degree that the study's findings are not statistically significant.

Several forms of extension neglect exist.

Scope Neglect or Scope Insensitivity

Scope neglect or *scope insensitivity* means that the larger a study, the less personal involvement people have in it. For example, researchers asked people how much they would pay to cover oil ponds so that birds do not become trapped in them. They had to provide a dollar amount for 2,000, 20,000, or 200,000 migrating birds. The amounts, at $80, $78, and $88 respectively, did not take into consideration the number of birds.

Psychologist Daniel Kahneman (1999) explained:

"The story...probably evokes for many readers a mental representation of a prototypical incident, perhaps an image of an exhausted bird, its feathers soaked in black oil, unable to escape,"

— PSYCHOLOGIST DANIEL
KAHNEMAN (1999)

---

and subjects based their willingness to pay mostly on that mental image.

Philosopher Toby Ord believes scope neglect explains why existential risks to humanity itself are often under-weighted:

We treat nuclear war as an utter disaster, so we cannot distinguish nuclear wars between nations with a handful of nuclear weapons (in which millions would die) from a nuclear confrontation with thousands of nuclear weapons (in which a thousand times as many people would die, and our entire future may be destroyed).

Duration Effect

Duration neglect is another specific form of extension neglect because it uncovers an anomaly in the way people judge an experience. This means that the way people judge how unpleasant or even painful an experience is has little to do with how long the experience lasted. Several experiments showed the judgements depend on two factors: the peak (when it was the most painful) and how quickly that pain goes away. If the pain goes away slowly, they judge the experience to be more painful.

This results in the *peak end rule*. What people remember about an experience is its peak, the most intense part, and its end. They do not base their judgement on the total sum or average of every moment. This occurs whether they have undergone a pleasant experience or an unpleasant one. They do not lose the information they have that does not include the peak or the end, but they do not use it.

People are most likely to misjudge the duration of an experience if it is unfamiliar to them. They find it easier to estimate how long a telephone rings, for example, or how long their commute to work takes. If they have a standard of comparison, they can also more easily estimate the length of an experience.

For example, they showed subjects pleasant and unpleasant film clips. Later, the researchers asked them to think about the clips and review them in their minds. Interviews with the subjects showed the subjects judged the clips like a series of snapshots they either liked or disliked. They did not seem to consider the length of the clips or factor that into their judgements (Fredrickson, B. and Kahneman, D., 1993).

Conjunction Fallacy

This fallacy derives from the likelihood of two traits occurring with one another is much less likely than simply accounting for one trait. Amos Tversky, one author of the most famous example of the fallacy, named their study after Linda Covington, his secretary at Stanford:

Linda is 31 years old, single, outspoken, and very bright. She majored in philosophy. As a student, she was deeply concerned with issues of discrimination and social justice, and also took part in anti-nuclear demonstrations.

Which is more probable?

1. Linda is a bank teller.
2. Linda is a bank teller and is active in the feminist movement.

Although most of the participants chose option 2, the probability of two events occurring together, in conjunction, always is less than or equal to the probability of either occurring separately. The authors believed people got the problem wrong because option 2 seemed more representative of Linda based on her description. Here, the probability of Linda being a bank teller is 0.05 and the probability of her being a bank teller and a feminist is 0.0475.

23

ZERO RISK

As explored in the chapter on loss aversion (Chapter 4), people are averse to any kind of loss and choose options with a lower risk when another option with higher risk might serve them better. The concept of zero risk explores this further. It turns out that people will make a suboptimal choice if the other choice offered them promises zero risk. This bias plays on the human fear of uncertainty. People want to know their future and attempt to eliminate all the known risks they can imagine happening so their future will be bright, full of success and accomplishments.

The zero risk bias is a cognitive bias that developed to reduce the stress involved in making choices. But when people decide on an option based on zero risk, they rarely quantify the risk when, if they did, they would clearly see that an option involving some risk is a better choice.

However, people are not calculators and most do not quantify all the probabilities involved in a choice. They usually decide depending on how they feel about the topic. Therefore, they may purchase an insurance policy that covers emergency surgery while abroad, even though the chance they will use such a policy is miniscule. What they are actually doing is buying peace of mind because they have eliminated one potential risk.

The concept of zero risk was first developed in 1987 when researchers asked participants how much they would pay to reduce the risk of suffering side effects from cleaning products. Respondents would pay up to three times more if they reduced the side effects from five of 15,000 to zero of 15,000. The other choice was a risk reduction from fifteen of 15,000 down to ten of 15,000. The reduction in risk compared to the first choice was statistically negligible (Viscusi, K., Magat, W. and Hubert, J.).

The Covid-19 Toilet Paper Run

Conditions during the Covid-19 pandemic have presented people with a lot of risk along with the difficulty of making choices when all the options seem to pose a risk. Making a quick trip to the store vs. staying home and paying $15 for a delivery. Sending children to school vs. keeping them home. Choosing to work from home when your presence in the office might mean a better chance at promotion.

The chance of running out of toilet paper does not seem all that serious compared to life-and-death choices people have had to make. But supplying oneself with this commodity meant they cut one risk down to zero. One compromise did not have to be made. The run on toilet paper during the early months of the pandemic is an example of the zero-risk bias in action, in which people tried to modify the stress of so much decision-making by having one item securely in hand, resulting in at least one item they didn't have to worry about.

The Allais Paradox

They named the Allais paradox after French economist Maurice Allais, who in 1953 laid it out as two options in an example of behavioral economics:

Option A: Win $100 million for sure
Option B: 10% chance of winning $500 million
89% chance of winning $100 million
1% chance of not winning anything at all

Although the expected value for Option B was far greater, people would routinely choose Option A. Under Option B they would probably win as much as in Option A but also had a great chance of winning five times as much, with only a sliver of risk they would win nothing at all.

Carbon Capture and Storage Risks

A solution to global warming called carbon capture also involves risks that the underground storage, which is in areas chosen by geologists, might leak. For that reason, negotiations undertaken by governments and their public have proven quite difficult.

Carbon capture is important because worldwide energy demand keeps expanding, and many products have to be manufactured using fossil fuels, like steel or cement. It is an interim stage before we develop the means to deliver totally clean energy. The carbon capture technology would capture carbon, transport it if needed, and store it miles underground. An impenetrable cap rock would cover the reservoir sites. Often workers would use the same reservoir that stored the oil.

The chance these reservoirs might leak is slim but not nonexistent. However, because of the zero risk bias, it is a possibility that looms large in people's minds. Failure to build carbon capture centers means facing the prospect of climate change, which is dire, but the public might favor it because they want to avoid any harm at any cost. Countries would have to cooperate for carbon capture to do much good, but the countries all have to decide on their own, and some of them might not want to take the risk of leakage, although such a risk is miniscule (Gavrilova, A.).

24

OSTRICH EFFECT

The ostrich effect is when people avoid negative information, even though knowing that information is essential for, or contributes to, a cherished goal. Social psychologists studying this effect first concentrated on investors in the stock market. They found investors better kept track of their investments when the market was going up. However, the same investors did not review this information during a bear market.

Regarding everyday financial problems, a British survey found that among people who were anxious about their finances, only ten percent actually looked at those finances at least once a month (Webb, T. L., Chang, B. P., & Benn, Y., 2013).

The ostrich effect can play a role in many types of human endeavor, not only investing and finance. People highly relate it to their need to protect their ego and continue to think highly of themselves, no matter how badly they are actually doing. Even though it would be beneficial to know this information so they could improve their performance or edge out of an unsuitable situation, they often cannot do so while keeping their heads in the sand, so to speak.

The ostrich effect is a type of cognitive bias, and it relates to several other such biases. especially cognitive dissonance (see Chapter 15). In fact, the ostrich effect may spring from cognitive dissonance: people refuse to take in information that contradicts their own view of the world and how they see themselves acting in the world. The ostrich effect also reinforces people's tendency to want to remain optimistic about things.

The Ostrich Effect and Climate Change

We may see the ostrich effect at work in some people's reaction to climate change. Despite all the scientific evidence that is out there and the evidence they can see for themselves, some people refuse to face this looming catastrophe. They deny climate change and refuse to pay for ways to mitigate it. In fact, in the United States, 18 percent of Americans believe (1) the climate is not changing or (2) human activity has nothing to do with it (Harvey, F., 2019).

Especially when the stakes are high, the ostrich effect is at work (such as the very survival of the Earth). This, of course, is a serious societal consequence, but the ostrich effect can have serious consequences for the individual as well, often affecting their health. One study found that 20 percent of people who had signed up for a weight loss program had never weighed themselves before. The same study found that most diabetics do not monitor their blood glucose levels despite the availability of inexpensive, pain-free methods now available to do so at home (Webb, T. L., Chang, B. P., & Benn, Y., 2013).

One study showed that the worse the news is about environmental issues, the more certain people wanted to avoid doing anything about it. Two groups of participants, one fairly knowledgeable about energy issues and the other less informed, read different passages about oil shortages. The knowledgeable people read a passage that predicted that the United States would have enough oil for 240 years, while those more ignorant of the topic read that the United States would run out of oil in 40 years. Both groups then completed a questionnaire on how much more they would like to learn about this problem. It turned out that the less knowledgeable people, who had read the most urgent passage about oil shortages, did not want to learn anything more about the issue. This finding suggests that as people become more cognizant of the threat posed by climate change, the less willing they will be to act to correct it (Shepherd, S., & Kay, A. C., 2012).

No Desire for Constructive Criticism

The ostrich effect is also highly related to loss aversion (see Chapter 24). People lose sight of their goals because it is painful to achieve them, and thus the ostrich effect kicks in as they simply refuse to take the necessary steps.Thus maybe a student's goal is to get an "A" in class, yet they routinely ignore their professors' suggestions for improvement on their college papers. The pain of knowing exactly what the professor thinks simply looms larger in their minds than the pride they will feel when achieving their goal.

This tendency can carry over into the workplace, where one essential ingredient for success is the ability to take constructive criticism from coworkers and bosses. When a person should ask for feedback, they do not because of their drive to protect their ego. Also, there are some work environments where workers are not in the habit of requesting feedback. This condition may hold back other workers from asking for the feedback because they worry other people might judge them harshly for doing so.

How People Avoid Information

People avoid information in several ways.

Physical avoidance. This is a way just to avoid the information. Important conversations that ought to take place do not happen. They never read certain newspapers or watch certain television or radio programs. Job ratings go right into the filing cabinet without being perused.

Inattention. If that TV show or radio program is on, they pay no attention to what is being said.

Biased interpretation of information. The person interprets information so that they can ignore any unpleasant implications.

Forgetting. The person may have processed the information but forgets it soon afterwards.

Self-handicapping. People avoid knowing about themselves and what gifts and talents they may actually have by choosing work that is too easy or too hard for them (Effectiviology).

Avoiding the Ostrich Effect

Sometimes, even though they know they are avoiding information on purpose, and even though the information might prove helpful or even necessary, people find it difficult to push through their barriers and confront the thing they fear. There are certain debiasing techniques they can use in this case. One is to create psychological distance from the problematic information. They can even pretend they are helping a friend, not themselves, when they look up the information.

Or, they might set up automated reminders like scheduled emails or notifications on their computer or phone that provide the information in a format they are likely to check. A time-honored way to keep promises to oneself is to have an accountability partner with whom they meet or whom they call at scheduled intervals. In the event they want to help another person with their finances or other issues, they can draw on these techniques.

Finally, people might try mindfulness exercises to help them stay focused on their long-term goals.

25

NAIVE REALISM

Naive realism, a cognitive bias, explains how people view the world from their own perspective while believing that everything they see is objective reality. Therefore, they do not see how biases are clouding their judgement and believe that other people who do not share their views must be irrational, ignorant, or biased. They think all others will arrive at their conclusions if the others have access to the same information and interpret it rationally. For this reason, people often project their own beliefs, feelings, and opinions onto others.

Because their own reactions to a certain situation seem unbiased and rational, people think that if others have different reactions to the same situation, they must be biased and irrational. If this happens often enough between a person belonging to a certain group and members of another group, the person can come to believe that the entire group is irrational and biased. These beliefs can stand in the way of any successful dispute resolution between the two groups.

Arab-Israeli Conflict

In a 1995 study on dispute resolution conducted by the Stanford Center on Conflict and Negotiation (SCCN), researchers considered institutional, strategic, and psychological barriers between the sides in the Arab-Israeli conflict. The authors attempted to answer this tough question:

Why do nations so often squander their resources and the lives of their citizenry in ruinous military ventures before coming to the negotiation table? Why, in short, do deadly conflicts and debilitating stalemates persist in the face of potential settlements that plainly would serve the interests of both sides? (Lee Ross and Andrew Ward)

What in their study they called "divergent construal" is like naïve realism: "Opposing partisans exposed to the same objective information are apt to interpret those facts differently." Lee and Ward found that polarization between parties exacerbates an inter-group conflict. Each side feels more sinned against than sinning. Both sides think they seek only what they believe is due to them. Each side may believe its interests are the ones that need the most protection under any agreement.

When a settlement agreement forces both sides to make concessions, each side views its own concessions as significant but minimizes any concessions the other side has to make. Both sides feel that they have made greater sacrifices than the other side and will deserve greater concessions in the future. As the researchers say:

Adversaries engaged in bargaining are apt to make overly uncharitable inferences about each other's offers and responses, seeing deviousness and intransigence by the other side, even when that side's offers, counteroffers, and expressions of disappointment and frustration are no less genuine than their own (Lee Ross and Andrew Ward).

Ross and Ward proposed that debriefing adversaries about the social and psychological processes that may hamstring their efforts to achieve a compromise may help them more easily achieve their goals.

Liberals, Conservatives, and Race Relations

Ross and Ward took part in another study in 1995, this one about how liberals and conservatives view social issues like abortion and race relations. For brevity's sake, I will focus on their findings on how naïve realism affects how the groups construe race relations in the United States.

They asked liberal and conservative participants, plus another group that claimed to be apolitical, all of them undergraduates at Stanford University, to interpret a court case involving the 1986 death of a young Black man, Michael Griffith, who was run over by a car while attempting to escape a White mob in the Howard Beach neighborhood of New York City.

What really stood out to the researchers was the way partisans and nonpartisans estimated this difference. They overestimated the extremity and ideological congruency of the other side and of their own side as well. Not only that, but all the groups perceived those holding the conservative less accurately, including their own, than those holding the liberal position.

What the study revealed was that participants "assumed that they alone proceeded from facts or reasonable factual assumptions, guided by reasonable ethical and philosophical principles, but untainted by ideological or political bias" (Robinson, R. J., Keltner, D., Ward, A., and Ross, L., 1995).

The participants believed they perceived the correct reality. They believed their opponents were operating from a subjective reality and that the way their opponents construed the evidence was also subjective.

The researchers believed that moderates within groups play a useful role because they can convince fellow partisans who are extremist to go beyond the rhetoric and posturing and consider underlying interest, assumptions, concerns, and any feelings of uncertainty or ambivalence the members may have. They advised vigilance in situations where people were not responding to actual views but to their wrongful assumptions about the other side's views and the character of those who hold those views.

26

SELF-SERVING BIAS

The self-serving bias has much in common with the fundamental attribution error (Chapter 19), where a person places blame on another while failing to account for the other person's situation. In the self-serving bias, a person places blame on another when things go south, but gives themselves the credit when they are successful.

This bias is not the same for everyone. Depressed people and older people are less likely to exhibit it— the depressed person because they always think they do everything wrong, and older people because of the benefit of their experience. They have a more balanced view of themselves and their abilities. Also, the bias shows up differently in different cultures: in individualistic, mainly Western cultures, people are more likely to have this bias than in collectivist cultures that mainly exist in the East. In relationships, it is interesting to note that men blame women more for problems in the relationship than women blame men. However, overall, women and men display the bias equally.

The list of scenarios where this bias might occur is endless, and it also exists in relations between nations. Many studies of the bias concentrate on athletes, who often brag about their prowess if they are winning, but will heap accusations on the umpire or referee if losing. After marriage, it may be at its most insidious in the workplace. Everyone hates the coworker who takes credit for the company's successes but blames others for its losses. If that person just happens to be the CEO, most likely the employees keep their opinions to themselves.

Loci of Control

How the self-serving bias affects or does not affect individuals depends on their locus of control. A person who believes their actions have led to a negative outcome is exhibiting an internal locus of control. A person who blames others for their mistakes has an external locus of control. People with an external locus of control are more suscep-tible to the self-serving bias.

People can change their locus of control. For exam-ple, if they have a quarrel with a friend, they might blame their friend. However, they could have changed their behavior. Changing the subject might have stopped the contre-temps. Or suppose they made a lousy investment. Instead of blaming terrible advice, they could have practiced due diligence in choosing an investment advisor.

Self-Esteem

To succumb to the self-serving bias is tempting because it does wonders for a person's self-esteem. Tests have shown that most people see themselves as "above average," which is impossible, as not everyone can be above average. People want to avoid the painful realization that they themselves might have something to do with that terrible debacle. It is so much easier to blame the other guy, the situa-tions, the weather, etc.—anything to prove that it is not their fault.

The ways the bias works to enhance self-esteem are (1) it helps a person believe they did their best and

(2) it is an attempt to maintain an image for others to notice.

The self-serving bias has some benefits. People feel more optimistic when they see themselves in a favorable light. They feel more inspired to accomplish something. If they noticed all their flaws, they might get bogged down in negativity and lose sight of their admirable qualities. However, the self-serving bias can lead to narcissism, conflict, and adverse relationships.

Another theory explaining the self-serving bias is its relationship to a person's expectations. If something turns out the way the person was expecting it to, the person attributes the outcome to internal factors. However, if the outcome is unexpected, the person relates it to external factors. And then there is the theory that points to the human being's natural proclivity for optimism. Negative outcomes are a surprise, so people are more likely to attribute them to external factors.

As Harvard undergrad Charlotte Ruhl (2021) proposed in a paper defining the self-serving bias, the two theories fit one another nicely:

"Because humans are naturally optimistic, we expect positive and successful outcomes, so when they don't occur we assume it results from situational factors alone."

— CHARLOTTE RUHL (2021)

How to Overcome It

The first step may be the hardest: awareness, which involves bringing what is unconscious into consciousness. And then, a little self-understanding and self-compassion. Biases developed for a reason —to think on one's feet and be able to make snap judgements and decisions. It is important to be able to recognize this bias when it shows up, because the only way people will really learn and grow is to learn how to be better at taking criticism. Mindfulness practices can help with self-acceptance—being able to love oneself despite the flaws.

27

BAADER-MEINHOF PHENOMENON

The human lives an illusory life, not a rational life. Such was the opinion of Arnold Zwicky, who in 2006 gave a formal name to the Baader-Meinhof phenomenon, a term that had been tooling around social media for several years. Zwicky called it "frequency illusion," and he listed it with several other illusions he had observed that made him throw up his hands in helpless frustration.

The leftist gang, Baader-Meinhof, created havoc in Germany (West Germany at the time of its founding) from 1970 to around 1998, when the third generation of the terrorists disbanded. They have nothing to do with the phenomenon that bears their name. It so happened that in 1994 a man named Terry Muller wrote a letter to a newspaper column had heard mention of the gang twice within a short span of time, which he thought was weird because the group was not making news by then, though it was still around, and so Muller had called this rather strange distortion of reality the "Baader-Meinhof Phenomenon."

I have dubbed it The Baader-Meinhof Phenomenon —named after the notorious West German gang of terrorists. The phenomenon goes like this: The first time you learn a new word, phrase or idea, you will see that word, phrase or idea again in print within 24 hours. (This does not apply to topical things—just obscure words, etc.)

As you might guess, the phenomenon is named after an incident in which I was talking to a friend about the Baader-Meinhof gang (and this was many years after they were in the news). The next day, my friend phoned me and referred me to an article in that day's newspaper in which the Baader-Meinhof gang was mentioned. *Quelle surprise!* [Bulletin Board noted, in 1994: You may recall that on two occasions, The Wordsmith of St. Paul reported seeing a word a second time within a day after first encountering it and looking it up – but he didn't give the phenomenon a cute name.]

Within my circle of friends, the expression 'Baader-Meinhof' is now well known—as in: 'I had the greatest Baader-Meinhof yesterday.' It instantly communicates this complex and puzzling experience of seeing something in print so soon after learning about it (Pioneer Press, 2007).

Now the definition has widened, so not only could a person see something in print that they have only recently noticed; they could see it everywhere. A good example of this is that when someone is considering purchasing a car, suddenly they spot that car everywhere: on the road, parked nearby, in a TV ad, cropping up in conversations.

Zwicky (2006) thought this illusion involved two cognitive biases: selective attention bias, followed by confirmation bias (Chapter 2). Selective attention starts because an unfamiliar word, thing, or idea intrigues a person; unconsciously, they watch for it and accordingly find it astonishingly often. Their confirmation bias acts as a reassurance that every time you see the thing, the more proof there is that it has suddenly become omnipresent.

Regarding the new car, first the person is blocking out other stimuli and concentrating on a possible acquisition, the car. Second, they are choosing to focus on that car and disregard any other information that they might have noticed at the time (like another model of car), or news that does not interest them, or a conversation that bores them.

Whatever has caught and kept their attention at that moment on an unconscious level must excite them or be important to them. For me, this happened when I noticed a word I had never seen before while reading a mystery—detritus. I suppose it was unusual because most mystery novels are not known for their evocative language. However, the author was P.D. James, now a Dame of the British Empire, and she could use any word she chose, I imagine. At any rate, she used that word a lot throughout the course of her book, and I noticed it every time. I was enjoying the mystery so I never looked up detritus, but later I found out it is a fancy term for garbage. And then even later I read an article about how some words come into style and then become overused, and one word the writer mentioned was detritus. So I am not sure if I only imagined I saw the word more often when I had not come across it before, or that certain authors had taken a liking to the word and so it was actually showing up more than before!

Swedish publicist Jerry Silfwer considered this likelihood—he called it a possible "butterfly effect:"

...we live in an interconnected society. We shouldn't underestimate the chaotic network effects.There's actually a possibility that your initial feeling indeed is right; a small spark could lead to a butterfly effect and increase the likelihood of you encountering the same thing soon again because of this spreading chain of events.

The Baader-Meinhof phenomenon is mostly harmless, but it could pose a threat to people with mental illness because it might increase their susceptibility to paranoia.

28

PLAN CONTINUATION BIAS

Plan continuation bias can explain the difficulty people have in giving up a plan already in place. This tendency to carry on with a plan that is leading nowhere or worse, leading to disaster, is like the sunk cost bias (Chapter 11). According to economists, people should not consider their sunk cost (what they spent in the past) when planning for the future, but this is hard advice for the average person to take. If they have spent $50 on a concert ticket but have come down with a cold, they will often still go, even if following through with their plan costs days off work because now they are really sick.

Plan continuation bias describes an ongoing phenomenon rather than considering decisions a person has already made. A person's grasp of a situation is gradually diverging from how the actual situation is playing out in the present moment. Primarily, this happens for two reasons. Early on, as the plan unfolds, the cues that it is a good plan and a safe one appear compelling. The plan has worked before. And then, there appear cues that the situation is changing, and not for the better, but these seem to be ambiguous, contradictory, and difficult to process. The person says to themselves, "Is this really what I think it is?" (WISEducation).

By that time, the person is married to their plan and finds it difficult to let go. They think that if they give it up now, that will make them look bad. So, as fresh problems arise, they just add more layers of complexity, and risk, to the original plan, when they should have reassessed the entire plan when the problems first arose.

Ships Staying the Course into Disaster

Failing to adjust your behavior to fit conditions has resulted in disasters in the transportation industry. Consider Captain Edward J. Smith of the *Titanic*, who retired to his stateroom while the ship traversed an ocean populated by icebergs.

Another well known shipping disaster involved the *Torrey Canyon*, which in 1967 was one of the largest oil tankers in the world. Here, the captain had a deadline to meet, and in order to do that, he had to beat the tide. To save time, he changed course on his way to the port in Wales. He chose the most dangerous of two channels, which would save a few hours, even though only ships much smaller than the *Torrey Canyon* used that channel.

The tides and a costly delay loomed in his mind, so when currents pushed the ship off course, he continued on. He kept on ordering tighter and tighter turns, while all that time currents pushed the ship even further off course. It may have been that the situation seemed ambiguous. His native optimism led him to believe they could push through. Eventually the ship foundered on an underwater rock and split in two, spilling a hundred million gallons of oil off the British coast. The disaster still ranks as one of the top ten oil spills in the world.

Could 19 Airline Crashes Been Avoided?

In 2004, the National Aeronautics and Space Administration (NASA) undertook a study of 19 airline crashes that took place in thunderstorms because of pilot error. In all the cases, the pilots could have diverted to another airport but did not. How to explain the pilots' decisions to press on in a worsening situation?

Among many other factors considered, the NASA study pointed to the ambiguous nature of the information available to the pilots who continued their approach near thunderstorms:

1. The guidance provided by the airline company was generic; they had no algorithm to calculate when to break off an approach.
2. The crew had to integrate fragmentary information to make their best judgement. They knew if they guessed wrong, they would shoulder the blame.
3. The crew's judgement may not have been that different from crews of airplanes that did not crash when in a similar situation.

NASA noted that penetration of storm cells happened often. Other flights may have landed or taken off without difficulty a minute or two before the flight that crashed. Also, the crews answered to the company, which wanted to keep costs down and passengers satisfied.

NASA realized that plan continuation bias was a factor in the crashes. They noted that the bias appears stronger as a person nears completion of an activity, like landing a plane. Also, the bias might have prevented the crews from noticing "subtle cues showing conditions have changed" (Dismukes, K and Loukopoulos, L., 2004).

Bias Workarounds in a Business Context

David Martin, a business coach, suggests that organizations pay special attention to their plans to make sure that a course of action is adaptive. They should put systems in place that have strong feedback loops. Whoever is in charge must have access to crucial information regularly throughout the duration of the project. Another way companies could "beat the bias" is to plan out an action in a series of short-term horizons. That way, decision-makers can check the current situation and assess the goals to see if they are still valid. Then they make a new plan for the next planning horizon.

29

THE GAMBLER'S FALLACY

The gambler's fallacy results from people refusing to believe in the total randomness of an event that is, by nature, random. They want to believe that past random events of the same nature also determine how that scenario will work out in the future. Though it can easily be applied to gambling (the belief in a "winning streak" or that on a certain day or time of day the gambler "cannot lose,"), it also shows up in other situations as well. Indeed, the fallacy was first described in 1820 when a French philosopher noted in an essay that men who wanted sons believed that each time their wife gave birth to a boy, the likelihood of the next child being a girl increased.

The fallacy is sometimes called the "Monte Carlo fallacy" because in 1913, gamblers at the Monte Carlo casino roulette wheel kept on betting on the red. The ball landed on the black time after time, so they reasoned that the next time it had to land on the red. In fact, the ball did not land on the red until the 27th time. By then, players had lost millions of dollars and the casino reaped a windfall. The chance of the ball landing on the black 26 times is about one in 66 million.

The gambler's fallacy occurs because human beings hate randomness, so they rationalize random occurrences by looking for patterns in the history of events that are similar. Also, people make judgements on samples that are too small to speak for the larger entity where the samples originated. When people use this to determine the likelihood of something happening, they often only choose the events they hope future events will bear a similarity to, or that would represent an ideal outcome. Last, people think about chance as something that is fair and balanced when it actually is not.

Investing and the Gambler's Fallacy

The tendency of investors to hold on to stocks that have depreciated and sell those that have appreciated is an example of the gambler's fallacy. Often they believe that when a stock is rising, it will soon crash, so to be on the safe side they better sell. They are making their decision in the belief that the price of the stock, which may be totally random, reflects the trend of its previous price points, but the two are not necessarily related. A stock's past price trajectory does not foretell its future performance (The Decision Lab).

Investors may see the stock market rise five days in a row and assume the streak cannot last forever. They may think on day six it will go down. Or, if the market has been a bear market for the past six months, they may believe it has to go up the seventh month. But, they should consider that rising markets may continue to rise and vice-versa. The confirmation bias may bolster their opinions (Chapter 2), in that they may only attend to news that confirms their beliefs.

Investors can fall prey to gambler's fallacy when looking at historical trends for a company or market. If they have a confirmation bias that backs up their "gut feeling," they'll make the wrong decision. If there is no rational basis for an investment decision, it is by definition a gamble. Financial markets are forward looking. Investors buy and sell based on expectations—not on winning or losing streaks, or on what has happened recently (iMoney Editorial, 2016).

Two Types of Gambler's Fallacy

Type I gambler's fallacy is where the gambler assumes that the roulette wheel is perfectly balanced and that each number is likely to occur. They keep track of outcomes on the sidelines and suddenly decide to bet because they think the random process has deviated too much. Type II is the gambler who watches the wheel while attempting to choose a favorable number. They have the erroneous belief regarding how many observations they will need to make to come up with that number. What they have failed to take into consideration is statistical power. This flaw in reasoning is common among social scientists, as reported by Jacob Cohen in 1988.

How to Avoid Gambler's Fallacy

The important thing for people to realize in countering gambler's fallacy is that the events they think are so predictable have no connection to one another. When a person has a vested interest in events being related somehow, it is not always easy to keep this in mind.

It may help to review the exact process by which the event is occurring and then to realize that the past events that bear resemblance to it actually have no role to play in its particular occurrence. Also, a person should consider the reasons they have for the past events to apply to the present event. When evaluating these reasons, they should leave out any role for chance or superstition.

Debiasing techniques that work by slowing down thinking and removing distractions when you are making a decision are also helpful in combating this fallacy. Because it is so common, a person is likely to come across it in others. The best way to deal with this is politely to show them that the events in question cannot possibly affect one another.

30

CURSE OF KNOWLEDGE BIAS

The curse of knowledge refers to the gap between those who know a great deal about a particular field and the people who need to know about the field but at present remain ignorant. Not everyone is a genius at teaching. They might have positions in business or conducting research and have no interest in or aptitude for instructing others. Or, they might be teachers of, say, seventh grade, or freshman subjects in high school or college. They do not know what their students do not know, and this can be a barrier to having a good relationship with the students.

The tools the knowledgeable employ to reach their audience may not fit the task at hand. They may rely on generalities or complex jargon that fly over their targets' heads. Take senior executives, for example. They and other managers have years of experience that they try to pack into one learning session, to little effect, because they have not come up with goals concrete enough for their staff to understand.

An executive or manager may try to rally the troops with a snappy slogan, such as "Being the best of the best," only to have it fall on deaf ears. What the executive does not realize is that when they and their marketing team came up with that slogan, it reflected their years of being immersed in business conventions. To them, the slogan summarizes all that they know. To the uninitiated, it may seem slightly ridiculous.

Instead, a more concrete slogan, such as "Leave nothing to chance," informs employees about the work they must accomplish.

Trader Joe's, a food retailer, claims to be "The home of cheap thrills," and it describes its target customer as an "unemployed college professor who drives a very, very used Volvo" (Heath, C. and Heath D., 2006). So, though its general goals statement is not all that different from similar outfits, when describing its business and its typical customers it is down-to-earth and specific.

Besides making it harder to teach or communicate their skills, the curse of knowledge also lessens the ability of the knowledgeable person to predict what less knowledgeable people will do. They forget that something that feels as natural as breathing to them is new to the other individual and may not realize how stressful it feels when exposed to something so unfamiliar. Also, the knowledgeable person may have expectations that the other person just cannot meet, adding to their stress.

Take learning to drive, for example. Whoever is teaching a teenager, perhaps a parent, does not expect her to press hard on the accelerator while reversing down a rough driveway in the middle of a snowstorm. But she does, and suddenly they have plowed through a snowbank and off the slightly elevated roadway. Luckily they are in the country, so she did not hit anyone. But there is no way that car will make it back onto the road without a tow truck. Back into the piano teacher's gothic farmhouse they tread, asking for use of the phone to call for help.

People afflicted with the curse of knowledge often cannot understand their past actions. They might beat themselves over the head for having done something foolish without cutting themselves some slack and realizing the decision they made at the time was correct, given what they knew then.

The Curse of Knowledge and Its Connection to Other Biases

In order to overcome the curse of knowledge, a person needs to know why it exists and its relationship to other common biases. One cause can be the habitual focus of the brain, which is to accrue knowledge. Other factors are the person's age and cultural background, which can influence people in the way and degree they display the curse of knowledge.

Some cognitive mechanisms also cause this bias.

Inhibitory control. When a person seeking to impart knowledge lacks this cognitive helper, it means that they cannot forget all that they already know in order to really understand another person's perspectives.

Fluency misattribution. Here, the expert is too optimistic that others already know the information they themselves already know and have processed. They assume that information they themselves possess is more commonly known by others than is the case. They have subjective fluency in the topic at hand, but think that the information is objective.

Anchoring and adjustment (Chapter 6). Here, when people consider the less-informed person's perspective, they struggle because they are starting from their own perspective and are then attempting to adjust their point of view to the other person's.

An Egocentric Bias

The curse of knowledge is a type of egocentric bias (Chapter 7) wherein a person relies too much on their own point of view, even when they attempt to understand the other person's point of view. Here, it works in a lopsided way because it influences only those who are trying to understand a less-informed perspective, not those trying to understand the more knowledgeable perspective.

The Curse of Knowledge in Teaching

When instructing adults or older teenagers, the teacher may be far too optimistic about what their students knew before entering the course. This is true especially when they are studying a highly specialized field that comes with loads of jargon to interpret. Not every teacher has an equal talent for simplifying language and making sense of impenetrable jargon. They may not have the ability or the time to engage in "upstream thinking" and put themselves in their students' shoes.

This can have unfortunate consequences for some students, who might be frightened away from a field because they cannot understand the teacher. And that type of work might suit them better than any other.

Ways to Avoid the Curse of Knowledge

First, it is important to understand the bias and the impact it might have on cherished goals. But, besides understanding the bias, it is crucial to continue to be aware of it and how it can foil good intentions. A leader, an executive, a team boss, or a teacher must keep in mind that others just are not all that familiar with what you do and the manner in which you do it. Of course, there may be more than one perspective involved, so it is important to get to know the individual who is attempting to learn something new, whether they be a staff member, a student, or an intern.

The curse of knowledge can also complicate personal relationships. A person may be angry at someone who has failed to apologize for something they did when the other person is not even aware they did it. It is important, therefore, to consider whether they indeed have that information. So in every case, identify what information the other person actually has and actually needs.

It is good to request feedback or, as a teacher, start out the school year testing your students so you know the breadth of their knowledge on a topic. In talking with someone about a complex topic ask them beforehand what they know about the topic to gauge their level of understanding. Then, err on the side of assuming they know less than that. Avoid using technical terms with newbies, particularly if the instruction is happening online and you cannot get feedback.

In selecting instructors for a particular training session, consider that the most expert of them may not be the best for that role. Being an expert could actually make them worse at teaching.

THE LAW OF SMALL NUMBERS

There aren't enough small numbers to meet the many demands made of them.

— RICHARD C. GUY (1988)

The "law" of small numbers is actually not a law, but a fallacy. It is the tendency of both experts and laypeople to assume that a small sample of a large population provides an accurate picture of that population. There is an actual law regarding the number of items in a sample, called the law of large numbers.

What this means is that there is a continuum of probability—the larger the sample drawn from the population is, the more likely it is to be accurate. Imagine that a miner working far up in the mountains finally is ready to sell his haul. He knows that, as usual, about half will be blue crystal and the other half gold nuggets. If he draws about 100 pieces from one of his panniers, more than likely about half will be crystal and the other gold. The odds are even more likely to be half and half if he dumps a thousand pieces onto a tarp on the ground to count them. Suppose, instead, that he draws out two pieces. Here, the odds are only fifty percent that half will be gold and the other half crystal. If he draws out one piece, the odds go down to zero.

This law, that large numbers fairly accurately reflect the population from which they are drawn whereas small numbers do not, poses a problem both in research and in everyday life. People think small samples will behave just like large numbers.

People have erroneous intuitions about the laws of chance. In particular, they regard a sample randomly drawn from a population as highly representative, similar to the population in all essential characteristics. The responses of professional psychologists to a questionnaire concerning research decisions illustrated the prevalence of the belief and its unfortunate consequences for psychological research (Tversky, A. and Kahneman, D., 1971).

Maternity Ward Example

In 1974, two psychologists whom we met in Chapter 4, Amos Tversky and Daniel Kahneman, who invented the term "the law of small numbers," tested how this "law" works when people make estimates. They proposed the following scenario to study participants: in a town with two hospitals, the smaller hospital reports that they have about 15 babies born each day, whereas the larger hospital has about three times as many—45 babies born every day. For a period during the year, the hospitals had to report the number of days boys outnumbered girls. On those days, though about 50 percent of each sex is born overall, in one hospital 60 percent of boys were born vs. 40 percent girls. Which hospital was it?

If people decided it was the larger hospital and most did, they had fallen prey to the fallacy. Because of the smaller number of births at the smaller hospital, there was more volatility in the sample, whereas that was not the case with the larger hospital. When you have a larger sample, it is less likely to stray from the 50 percent mean and thus will more accurately reflect the actual situation.

The law of small numbers is a heuristic, a term also first used by Tversky and Kahneman. So it is a mental shortcut making it easier for people to form judgements under uncertain conditions. It is an example of a representational heuristic. People using a representational heuristic use any generalizations of similar events that come easily to mind when assessing probabilities. Another example of the representativeness heuristic is the gambler's fallacy (Chapter 29).

Errors by Experts

In 1971, Tversky and Kahneman considered how experts in their own field of psychology often "live by" the law of small numbers. They analyzed questionnaires about research that respondents filled out and concluded that psychologists often gamble with their hypotheses when they rely on small samples. Psychologists, they found, have too much confidence in the early trends that show up in their studies and overestimate their significance. They think their results are replicable when they may not be and fail to attribute deviations to sampling variability.

Tversky and Kahneman did not claim their own sample was representative; they presented the questionnaire to a general session of the American Psychological Association and also to audiences at a mathematical psychology meeting. However, they expressed consternation that so many experts in their fields had so much belief in the law of small numbers. They thought this mistaken reliance on instinct could only be corrected if journal editors insisted authors adhere to norms regarding sample size when relying on statistics.

A Useless Study and Useless Results Costing More than $1 Billion

A sample that is too small exhibits more volatility with both positive and negative results. Rural counties in the United States show both the fewest rates of kidney cancer and the highest rates of kidney cancer because they do not compare in population to other sections of the country. Therefore, both results will occur depending on the study.

The Gates Foundation undertook a $1.7 billion study that showed that smaller schools rank higher in the list of the most successful schools than larger schools, because it ranked the schools by the most successful schools. In this ranking, the smaller schools were overrepresented near the top of the list. The money the foundation spent went toward creating smaller schools, sometimes splitting larger schools in half to prove this point.

However, none of the spending was necessary because, if you ranked the schools by which one performed badly, the smaller schools also appeared near the top of the list. Both findings result from the law of small numbers; smaller groups will land near the extreme ends of the spectrum.

Sports Betting

When sports betters mistakenly rely on the law of small numbers, they are usually finding patterns where none actually exist. When charts show winnings rising with a five percent yield, betters find it hard to believe that the winning sequence happened only by chance.

If a basketball player makes several baskets in a row, betters will assume they are "hot." But here the sample size is small—only nine players—and so it is not surprising that such a coincidence could happen. Scientists examining the shooting patterns of professional players found that a "hot hand" does not exist in basketball. The increased likelihood of a player making a shot after a previous shot than after missing a shot is up for grabs.

Sports bettors may use this bias to their advantage by locating teams that in their previous game exceeded expectations anyone had of them and bet against them in the next game they play. How this makes a person money if they lose is that the odds shifted toward over-performing teams. The only way to combat the shift is to go the other way.

Gamblers are making a mistake when they believe that a team's score is too high and so they bet against the team. Or, the other way, if they think the number is too low, they will place their bet on that team. They should do the opposite and bet with the house. This is because those making up these sports books know that when the numbers are noticeably too low or too high, most of the betting public is going to favor the under and vice-versa. "This is where the 'fade the public'" mentality... comes into play" (Booker, J., 2020).

32

SOCIAL PROOF

When people are free to do as they please, they usually imitate one another.

— ERIC HOFFER

The social proof principle is a deeply rooted, unconscious bias that can have good or bad effects, depending on the context. It is how people follow others' example, especially when they are uncertain of what they should do next. Its reason for being lies in antiquity, when humans first roamed the plains of Africa. A group of people see a lion coming toward them, so they run. But there is one person who does not follow the others. That person is no longer in the gene pool, and a bias is gradually born.

The principle truly takes hold when something—a fashion, a movie, an actor, a product—becomes popular. In this way, it is like the bandwagon effect (Chapter 20). The social proof principle is exactly that—it is a rule people follow when deciding what is socially correct behavior. People view an action as correct in a situation to the degree they see others performing it (Cialidini, R. B., 2021).

Social proof works fairly well because when many people do something, it usually is the correct way to proceed. Imitating the crowd helps people guard against costly social errors. As a shortcut, it is convenient for a person to know the correct way to behave in a new situation.

However, taking social proof as valid can also lead to costly errors because at times, the evidence people see is misleading or even false. Advertisers seek to use social proof to their advantage by asserting inflated claims about a product they wish to sell. The endorsements they point to in print ads and on TV may be false, and their evidence may be partial or fake, such as nightclub owners hiring people to stand in line outside the club to show how "popular" their venue is. Even in church, ushers sometimes salt collection baskets to show that most people are giving, and giving a lot.

Social proof can work in positive ways as well. It turns out that during COVID, the greatest determinant of people wearing masks was seeing others wearing masks. If customers believe online reviews are valid, a majority of them base their purchases on these reviews.

For environmental action, social proof's positive effects are at work both on the individual and institutional levels. People are more likely to do such environmentally positive things as recycle or compost if they see most of their neighbors doing so. One way nations have used social proof to encourage firms to follow environmental regulations is to rate all the polluting firms on their environmental efforts and then publish the results. Heavy polluters changed their ways when they saw how their poor performance compared to other companies' successful efforts (Cialidini, R. B., 2021).

Plural Ignorance

Whenever a person is unsure of themselves or finds themselves in a situation where everything seems unclear, that is when they will be most likely to turn to others for guidance. This urge is particularly strong when the situation involves a great many people.What the person may overlook is that the others are probing for social evidence as well. This is called "plural ignorance," and it can lead to tragic situations.

Reports on the murder of Kitty Genovese late at night in a well-lit New York neighborhood led many to castigate the people who looked down at the scene from apartment windows and did nothing to help. Although the reports may or may not have been true, the incident did lead to studies on whether bystanders will lend help in an emergency.

What can happen is that all the bystanders feel uncertain and wonder how to react. They look to others for hints of what to do and notice that no one else is doing anything, so they also do nothing. So many questions and explanations run through their minds. A person lying in the alley may have just suffered a heart attack and need a doctor. Perhaps it is a drunk sleeping off late-night carousing. Describing a hypothetical situation, Cialidini writes:

Because we all prefer to appear poised and unflustered among others, we are likely to search for that evidence placidly, with brief, camouflaged glances at those around us. Therefore, everyone is likely to see everyone else looking unruffled and failing to act. As a result, and by the principle of social proof, the event will be roundly interpreted as a nonemergency.

People will help almost one hundred percent of the time if they are certain that what they are seeing is an emergency. They do not help because they are unsure, not unkind. If someone finds themself in an emergency situation in a crowd, the best way to get help is to be specific as to who should help by pointing to a particular person and asking them to call 911.

Social Proof in "The Many"

When several people take part in a behavior, that becomes social proof for others around them, who start behaving the same way. One example is a lone person standing on a crowded sidewalk, staring up at the clear, empty sky. People walking by will pay them no heed. But, if the person invites several friends along to take part in the experiment, soon a large crowd will surround them, all looking upward. Passersby, trying to ignore the strange scene, will not be able to resist a brief glance upward.

Animals, like the humble fruit fly, also depend on social proof to adjust their behavior. Experimenters dyed a few of the male flies blue, and when the female fruit flies saw other females mating with the blue males, they copied that behavior 70 percent of the time (Cialidini, R. B., 2021).

A Facebook post that women in Baltimore risked abduction by a person or persons driving a white van caused havoc in the city when it went viral. Cialidini mentions the Facebook algorithms that caused widely shared posts to figure prominently in people's feeds as responsible for the panic. The Boston mayor issued a warning on TV, not on advice of the police but because "it was on Facebook" (For more about Facebook and other social media, see Chapter 33). As a result, an innocent man who owned a white van was shot to death, and another man lost his job.

It's telling that perceived validity of the rumor developed from unfounded fears, rendered contagious by the algorithms of a frequently checked social-media feed. "Truth" was established without physical proof; there was only social proof. That was enough, as it often is (Cialidini, R. B., 2021).

Another reason people turn to social proof to show them how best to behave is that if they see others doing something, they think it is feasible. For example, if they get a message telling them that if they reduce energy usage, they would save money on their next power bill, they might not imagine how this could happen. But a message telling them that many of their neighbors conserve energy in their homes is more understandable, and they believe if the neighbors can do it, so can they.

Social proof also resonates with people because it reinforces their need to belong, to be one among the many. As we learned in the chapter on cognitive dissonance (see Chapter 15) holding two ideas at the same time creates psychological distress. To avoid this, people decide it is better to agree with the group and just go along. The need to gain social acceptance and escape rejection are among the reasons cults exist and can recruit so many members. They retain members by initially showering them with affection. The threatened withdrawal of that affection causes people to remain in the group.

Jonestown Mass Suicide

The 1977 mass suicide of Jim Jones and his followers in Guyana may be the most hideous form of group-think in modern times. The murder of a congressional representative, three of his aides, and an ex-cult member when they tried to leave the compound convinced Jones he would soon be arrested and The People's Temple disbanded. He therefore did the unthinkable by convincing members to commit suicide, and the way this took place shows just how powerful the social proof bias can be.

Jones founded The People's Temple in San Francisco but had members in Los Angeles and in his home state of Indiana whom he encouraged to move to San Francisco. The congregation was multi-racial and most lived a communal lifestyle. They had given up everything to join The Temple, including their homes and their pets, which, sadly, were killed and buried in a mass grave. Jones had strong ties to the Black community and the Black press, which he used to publicize how the Temple cared for the poor.

Not just anyone could walk into The Temple. Members met visitors at the door and asked them to wait in the vestibule until they vetted them. They kept the unwelcome cooling their heels for hours until they gave up and left.

Jones feared the interference of the U.S. government, particularly the CIA. He moved the cult to Guayana to avoid any meddling with the authoritarian manner in which he ruled every aspect of members' lives. Given this attitude, the murder of representatives from the U.S. government was not surprising, but it had dire consequences.

But moving the group to Guyana had other implications besides escaping U.S. government surveillance. In this atmosphere, Jones wielded more power than ever before. He already had a group of compliant individuals, numbering about a thousand souls. Then add to that the sense of uncertainty these people must have felt. Here they were, in a rainforest, the likes of which they never encountered before, surrounded by people with whom they had nothing in common. When Jones called them together, showed them the vat of poisoned strawberry lemonade, and commanded them to drink it, they must have looked around, searching for cues about how to act in this situation. Their deep sense of uncertainty would have caused them to look for social proof about how they should act.

As in most cults, Jones had some extremely devoted followers who obeyed his every command. The members watched a young woman calmly step forward and have her baby sip a cup of the lemonade before drinking it herself, and then calmly walk over to a field and sit down. They watched her and the baby go into convulsions and die within four minutes. Everything seemed so calm and orderly. This must be the way to do it: stay calm, take turns, drink the lemonade, and walk over to the field to die. And so they did. Social proof followed to the nth degree.

So, why is this behavior not more common? Are there not many such cults, most with charismatic leaders and devoted followers to hang on the leaders' every word? Cialidini (2021) theorizes that Jim Jones' dynamism and charisma were not the key drivers of his followers' demise in such a shocking way. Instead, it was their move to Guyana a year prior to the suicide that made them susceptible to his deadly order. Being torn from their familiar surroundings, however depressing their circumstances were, caused them to be in an extreme state of uncertainty and this influenced them to follow the young woman and her baby to their deaths.

The lesson from this tragedy is to never underestimate the power of these unconscious biases. A few people escaped. Somehow, they could slow down their thinking and realize the gravity of their situation. In the conclusion to this book we will discuss fast and slow thinking and ways to escape the hold various biases have over human behavior.

33

FEAR OF MISSING OUT (FOMO)

The term "fear of missing out" (FOMO) made its debut in 1996 when an expert in brand development coined it to describe ebbing brand loyalty among consumers (Herman, D., 2000). This bias has existed in humans for quite a while, however; writers of many eras have described feelings of being left out, and most likely anxiety about being on the outside looking in cropped up before any written language could record it.

If there were a scale tracing the very beginnings of the written word until today, most likely social media sites such as Facebook and Instagram would be mere scratches on the graph, but many people today have never known a world without them. Recently, social scientists of all stripes have been examining the influence these sites have on society and have uncovered many negative consequences to the people they hold in thrall.

For example, Volkan Dogan in the *Journal of Cross-Cultural Psychology* explored how self-perception and self-concept contribute to FOMO. They concluded that:

The fear of missing out is intimately connected to the ways that individuals understand and experience the world—and what they feel they're being excluded from. By highlighting the connection between self-perception on social media and FOMO, Dogan illustrated why some experience this unique form of online exclusion (King Universities Online).

Scott Pelley, on *60 Minutes* (2021), devoted a major segment and several overtime segments to the effects of Facebook, Instagram, and other social media platforms on society. Sad to say, many of the people he and his interviewee, former Facebook staffer Francis Haugand, discussed are teenagers, some who will be the future leaders of Planet Earth.

But a leader in the making may die on the vine, through suicide, especially if the person is a girl.

Facebook's own internal documents show this to be true. FOMO becomes so intense for them they do not want to live any longer. They feel they are missing out on something so important that they question their own worth, their own value.

The more girls feel depressed, the more they use social media sites. As for boys, anxiety also drives them to use the sites more often. For almost all teenagers, when they use smartphones to access these sites, they have an even more intense FOMO, and they also fear others' evaluations of them, whether positive or negative. The smartphone usage turns their mood even darker. A Scottish study found that teenagers also are anxious because they feel they have to be available all the time; the social media world is a fast-paced world. The same study, by the University of Glasgow (2016) found that teenagers plagued by FOMO also have trouble sleeping.

However, people of all ages experience FOMO. It is linked to greater smartphone and social media usage, and researchers do not associate the findings with age or gender (Wolniewicz CA, Tiamiyu MF, Weeks JW, Elhai JD., 2017). Smartphone and social media usage can turn into a vicious cycle for everyone. FOMO can cause a person to need to engage with social media when social media is making them more and more depressed, a "negative, self-perpetuating cycle" (Scott, E., 2021).

Going through the social media posts on their phone, tablet, or computer, people start feeling envious and depressed. Someone is on a great vacation. Someone has a handsome boyfriend or pretty girlfriend. Someone just bought a new house, or a horse, or a car. Their children are cuter than mine. Someone is slimmer than me, prettier than me, more handsome than me, more desirable than me. What they seem not to realize at the time is that they are comparing what is going on in their perhaps rather dull life with all its daily routines to the *highlights* of someone else's life. In photographs, even facial features can appear more desirable through a trick of the light or carefully applied make-up. What cannot change is how heavy a person may be. Girls claim Instagram worsens their own body image, yet they cannot not look (*60 Minutes*, 2021).

Since a person is viewing only the highlights from someone else's life, they no longer know what is normal and think they are doing worse than their peers. Sometimes people they know are enjoying fun times without them. In earlier generations, knowing that one is an outsider was never so clear. FOMO can cause people to feel that their needs are not being met and simply becoming less satisfied with their life.

Phubbing and Teenagers (And Anyone Else Who Does It)

Besides FOMO, another term is cropping up when people write about social media these days: "phubbing." The word is a combination of "phone" and "snubbing," and it refers to the times almost every person alive (I have no exact statistics on this) finds themself in an intimate conversation with a friend, pouring their heart out, and suddenly the friend's smartphone rings, or a text comes in, and they occupy themselves with whatever they are seeing or hearing on the phone, totally ignoring their friend. Yes, there could be a family emergency. Yes, they forgot their kid, stranded at school, but otherwise most writers label this behavior as extremely rude and very disruptive to actual, genuine relationships.

I mention this because the study, released by our government's National Institute of Health (2018), considers both FOMO and phubbing as problematic social media use (PSMU) and refers to both of them when drawing from a large-scale survey study of 2663 Flemish teenagers. The researchers found that fear of missing out "was a positive predictor of both how frequently teenagers use several social media platforms and of how many platforms they actively use" (Franchina, V., Vanden Abeele, M. van Rooij, et al., 2018).

In 2015, Instagram overtook Twitter as a popular site around the world; the two most popular sites were Facebook and YouTube. The researchers noted that may be because, when people want to present themselves, pictures are more effective than words. Researchers chose Flemmish teenagers because in Flanders, nonprofits have banded together to conduct annual surveys on the use and ownership of digital media by Flemmish youth. The teenagers with FOMO used more private platforms, like Facebook and Snapchat, rather than more public ones, such as YouTube or Twitter.

Fear of missing out is a powerful predictor of social media usage, especially on sites where people have their own private networks, as with Facebook and Instagram. The researchers found strong correlations between FOMO and both using social media more frequently and using several social media accounts instead of just one or two. As revealed in the *60 Minutes* interview, the researchers found that the more teenagers check their accounts and find events they are missing out on, the more problematic their social media usage becomes.

The anxiety they feel leads them to depend on their smartphones, so they can check their accounts no matter where they are. This practice leads to "phubbing," described above. Phubbing can wreak havoc with friendships, because the teens are so eager to check their accounts that they "phub" the friend sitting right across from them. Thus, the teen with FOMO becomes even more isolated and anxious.

Ways to Counter FOMO

Someone who thinks they may be addicted to social media and that what they see online is making them sadder and more anxious may want to try several remedies suggested on the Verywell site. They might try:

Changing focus. This alludes to ways to adjust their own social media sites by weeding out the "friends" who brag and having more positive people contribute to their feed. People should ensure their feed shows posts that contribute to their wellbeing and feel good about themselves.

Keeping a Journal. This refers to how many "likes" a person gets on what they share online. Perhaps they can take their posts offline and have them be their own private journal reflecting their best memories. Keeping a journal can help you shift your focus from public approval to private appreciation of the things that make your life great. This shift can sometimes help you get out of the cycle of social media and FOMO.

Seeking Real Connections. When a person feels lonely, their emotions signal they need more and better connections in their life. But seeking them online may be harmful. Instead, try to meet up with someone in person. Meeting up with a friend or arranging an outing will provide a change of pace. Or just connecting with one person on social media can help make the connection more intimate.

Focusing on Gratitude. Keeping a gratitude journal can work wonders in changing a person's mindset. A good practice is also to tell others how much they appreciate them. When a person realizes how much they already have, they may not "go down the rabbit hole of social networking and FOMO" (Verywell).

34

THE LOLLAPALOOZA TENDENCY

The Lollapalooza Tendency is the "Confluence of psychological tendencies in favor of a particular outcome."

— CHARLIE MUNGER

What happens when more than one bias comes into play at crucial moments? Charlie Munger, storied investor and vice chairperson of Berkshire Hathaway, the conglomerate controlled by Warren Buffett, called this the "Lollapalooza effect." In considering this effect on human behavior, the key word is "confluence." While one bias might not be successful in steering someone to take action, several biases acting together probably will.

During the 1995 speech at Harvard Business School where he introduced this concept, Munger complained that the combined effect of many biases has been little studied:

The psychology people couldn't do experiments that were four or five things happening at once because it got too complicated for them and they couldn't publish. So they were ignoring the most important thing in their own profession. And of course the other thing that was important was to synthesize psychology with all else. And the trouble with the psychology profession is that they don't know anything about "all else."

The combination of biases can be positive, or negative, but together they are powerful drivers of behavior. Munger's example came from bidders' behavior during an auction, which is analogous to traders' behavior in the stock market. First, they think, "I should bid because they invited me to the auction (reciprocity: see Chapter 12); I said I would bid, so now I must (consistency, or anchoring, Chapter 6); I am already bidding; I must continue to bid (commitment tendency or loss aversion, Chapter 4) and this is a good thing I am doing because all my peers are doing it (social proof, Chapter 33)."

With investing, the Lollapalooza tendency can cause investors to act like a herd, buying in one sector and selling off a second. When there are too many moving pieces, a situation can become volatile. In such a situation, it becomes difficult to predict the outcome and a wise investor would hold off until things calm down. Also, when an investor wants to be sure that the Lollapalooza effect does not influence their actions, they should keep in mind their initial assumptions and then go through a mental checklist, ticking off the biases that might affect their decision.

The Subprime Mortgage Crisis of 2007-2008

The Lollapalooza effect magnified the subprime mortgage crisis of 2007-2008 and brought the global economy to its knees. This happened after Wall Street traders could now sell mortgages on the financial markets and, because they no longer kept the loans in-house, lenders became less concerned about a buyer's creditworthiness. Brokers and real estate agents forged ahead, offering deals they knew were risky, especially for buyers, and could hurt their company's reputation in the long run. They just wanted to make more money (Egocentric Bias, Chapter 7).

Borrowers jumped on the bandwagon—everybody was buying a house (social proof, Chapter 33) and with the more lenient regulations, they could too (bandwagon effect Chapter 20). They would take out loans to support unsustainable lifestyles, or speculate on real estate prices, figuring housing pricing would continue to rise. No one was thinking about the long-term consequences of their actions and as a result the mortgage market eventually collapsed.

The Rationale Behind Multi-Level Marketing and Direct Selling

Amway, Avon, MaryKay, Tupperware (the longest-lived of the bunch), all rely on regular people to sell their products in multi-level marketing endeavors. This approach takes advantage of several behavioral biases. Thus, they are attempting to increase sales by taking advantage of the Lollapalooza effect.

First, when an invitation arrives to attend such a gathering, people are already biased toward going because they know and like the person who invited them. Often, the party starts with a game; everyone gets a prize at the end of the game. Here, the recip-rocation bias comes into play. The person feels the need to pay back the ones who gave them a free item. The host or hostess asks old customers to talk about how good the product is, and this unleashes the commitment bias. Last, the person sees others purchasing these products. Since these people are their peers, often similar to them. This provides the needed social proof the product must be good.

Many people risk losing a friendship by refusing to attend such events; they know if they go, they will buy.

Positive Examples of the Lollapalooza Effect

Some positive events come to mind when considering the positive effects of the Lollapalooza tendency. One is the eradication of tuberculosis, which occurred only by combining drugs so that they worked in unison against the disease. Another is AA and its sibling organizations. Social proof and the bandwagon effect may be the biases that help account for its successes when nothing else has worked.

CONCLUSION

Many writers and psychologists concur that the best way to mitigate the effect of biases is to "slow down your thinking." Interestingly enough, in 2011, Daniel Kahneman, who with his colleague Amos Tversky described many of these biases for the first time, published *Thinking Fast and Slow* that explains how "slow thinking" can curb biases sometimes but not always. Kahneman divides cognitive performance into two types, System 1 (intuition, including biases) and System 2 (planned, logical functioning).

Usually, System 1 works just fine when navigating life's everyday challenges. A person can drive and carry on a conversation. They can read to a child but be thinking of something else. They are relying on long-established reflexes that just make everyday life a little easier.

Where they run into difficulties is when the problems they face are harder to navigate. They either stay in System 1 or can navigate to System 2. So often when faced with this dilemma, people stay under the calmer, gentler sway of System 1 rather than figure out the roadblocks ahead using System 2.

System 1, the system that produces the shortcuts as biases or heuristics that we have been discussing, works well until it does not. When things get sticky, a bias may lead a person to make the wrong choice.

People point to extraordinary feats of logic that appear to work instantaneously to support their claim that a person can accomplish great things using their intuition. They cite examples like an expert diagnostician who can enter a treatment room and tell what ails a patient with one penetrating glance. A chess master who stays three moves ahead of their less skilled opponent. However, these people's brains work differently from that of most of humanity. They get subtle cues from the situation, which give them access to a memory that provides them with the answer (Simon, 2002).

System 1 is constantly seeking coherence. If a person's System 2 is lazy, it will endorse many beliefs that are intuitive and reflect impressions made by System 1. Thus, a person's behavior can become biased without them ever knowing it. People jump to conclusions because they believe that what they see is all there is. Their System 1 "is radically insensitive to both the quality and the quantity of the information that gives rise to impressions and intuitions" (Kahneman, D., 2011).

It turns out that in many situations, people's logical, orderly System 2 can be just plain lazy and prone to accept the first, biased answer that occurs to it. This can lead to overconfidence. Psychological research has revealed that people in positions of power are overconfident when deciding upon new projects. Sometimes, as with the Concorde airliner (see Chapter 11), these projects overrun their estimated costs by millions, or even billions, of dollars.

One proposal to nip overconfident projections in the bud is to conduct a "pre-mortem." A group of knowledgeable individuals gathers to listen to a brief speech, such as, "Imagine that we are a year into the future. We implemented the plan as it now exists. The outcome was a disaster. Please take 5 to 10 minutes to write a brief history of that disaster" (Kahneman, D., 2011). By writing things down, people can notice their unconscious biases.

For ordinary people and experts attempting to make decisions outside their field, the biased choice is the path of least resistance. Often when a person makes it, they do so unconsciously because System 1 operates automatically. Therefore, they find it difficult to avoid errors of intuitive thought. To make decisions logically, they would have to turn to System II, but the problem is that this conscious, logical thinking part of the brain often remains unaware that an error has even been committed. As Kahneman observes,

The best we can do is a compromise: learn to recognize situations in which mistakes are likely and try harder to avoid significant mistakes when the stakes are high. The premise of this book is that it is easier to recognize other people's mistakes than our own.

It is impossible for the brain to remain vigilant all the time. When people face a demanding situation or must solve a knotty problem, the work that the brain does manifests itself physically. Kahneman and his co-researchers conducted several studies to show the impact of mental labor on the body. In one study, they measured people's pupils when engaged in solving a problem and discovered that their pupils always contract. In another study, they asked people to watch a film of a woman being interviewed and attend to her body language while ignoring words flashing across the screen. The researchers knew from prior experiments that the participants would suffer from ego depletion and would need glucose to keep up their strength to continue to do mental work. They gave one group lemonade sweetened with sugar, while the other got lemonade sweetened with a sugar substitute. Participants then embarked on a task where they had to overcome an intuitive response to get the correct answer. Those who drank the Splenda-sweetened lemonade made the most errors during the second task.

When people only hear one side of an argument, when they believe that what they see is all there is, they often feel more confident in their judgement because they have heard a coherent story that makes sense to them. They can make easy judgments when they only know part of the story and do not suffer cognitive dissonance (see Chapter 15). The bias often works well for people. It explains why humans can think fast and make sense of partial information in a complex world. But relying on partial evidence can also lead to overconfidence, to the framing effect (see Chapter 21), and to errors in logic that cause a person to overlook sample size (see Chapter 22). Also at play here are the halo effect (see Chapters 9) because important qualities a person may lack effectively to complete a task have been overlooked in favor of a brilliant first impression.

System 2, the logical system, tries to find answers to any questions it may generate or be presented with, whereas System 1 is continuously monitoring everything going on outside and inside the mind and continuously generating assessments with no specific intention and little or no effort. Then, System 2 may substitute such basic assessments for more troublesome questions because

---

"we have inherited the neural mechanisms that evolved to provide ongoing assessments of threat level, and they have not been turned off"

— (KAHNEMAN, D., 2011)

In order to block the errors generated by System 1, a person must recognize that they are in a "cognitive minefield, slow down, and ask for reinforcement from System 2" (Kahneman, D., 2011). Therefore, the best way to deal with intuitive biases is to know more about them, and that is the purpose of this book.

REFERENCES

Allais, M. (1953). "Le comportement de l'homme rationnel devant le risque: critique des postulats et axiomes de l'école américaine." *Econometrica: Journal of the Econometric Society*, 503-546.

Anissimov, M. "What are Halo Effects?" *InfoBloom*. www.infobloom.com

Arkes, H. R., and Ayton, P. (1999). "The sunk cost and Concorde effects: Are humans less rational than lower animals?" *Psychological Bulletin*, 125(5), 591-600. https://doi.org/10.1037/0033-2909.125.5.591

Best, M. and Newhauser, D. (2004) "Heroes and Martyrs of Quality and Safety: Ignaz Semmelweis and the birth of infection control." *BMJ Journals: BMJ Quality and Safety. www.bmj.com.* Qual Saf Health

Care 2004;13:233–234. doi: 10.1136/qshc.2004.010918.

Bibas, S. (2004). "Plea Bargaining outside the Shadow of Trial." *Harvard Law Review,*117(8), 2463. doi:10.2307/4093404

Bloom, S. (2021) "The Cognitive Bias Handbook: Part II: The Ben Franklin Effect, the Ikea Effect, and More." *The Curiosity Chronicle.* www.sahilbloom.substack.com

Bobo, J. (2020) "The Availability Bias: "Why We Worry In Our Remarkably Safe World." *Futurity: where food meets the future. www.futurityfood.com*

Booker, J. (2020) "Sports Betting Biases to Use to Your Advantage." Best US Casinos. www.BestUS-Casinos.org

Buchdahl, J. "The law of small numbers in sports betting." *Pinnacle.* www.pinnacle.com

Boyce, P. (2020) "Hindsight Bias Definition and Examples." *BoyceWire.* www. BoyceWire.com

Campbell, S. D. and Sharpe, S. A (2007) "Anchoring Bias in Consensus Forecasts and its Effect on Market Prices." Finance and Economics Discussion Series Divisions of Research & Statistics and Monetary Affairs Federal Reserve Board, Washington, D.C. www.federalreserve.gov.

Castano, E., Martingano, A. J., Perconti, P., (2020) "The effect of exposure to fiction on attributional complexity, egocentric bias and accuracy in social perception." Plos One. https://doi.org/10.1371/journal.pone.0233378

Cherry, K, (2021) "The Dunning-Kruger Effect." *Verywellmind.* www.verywellmind.com

Cialidini, R. B. (2021) *Influence, New and Expanded: the Psychology of Persuasion.* Harper Business. (Kindle Edition) Harper Collins Publishers, New York.

Cohen, J. (1988) Statistical Power Analysis for the Behavioral Sciences Second Edition. Department of Psychology New York University New York, New York.www.toronto.edu

Cuncic, A., ed. Swaim, E. (2021) "The Spotlight Effect and Social Anxiety: Not Everyone Is Staring at You." *Verywell Mind. www.verywellmind.com*

The Decision Lab. "Why do we buy insurance? Loss aversion, explained." The Decision Lab. www.The-DecisionLab.com

The Decision Lab. "Why do we feel more strongly about one option after a third one is added? The Decoy Effect, explained."www.thedecisionlab.com

The Decision Lab. "Why do we make worse decisions at the end of the day? Decision Fatigue, explained." The Decision Lab. www.TheDecision-Lab.com

The Decision Lab. "Why do we place disproportionately high value on things we helped to create? The IKEA Effect, explained." *The Decision Lab.. IKEA effect - Biases & Heuristics | The Decision Lab*

The Decision Lab. "Why do we think a random event is more or less likely to occur if it happened several times in the past? Gambler's Fallacy, explained." www.thedecisionlab.com

Dismukes, K and Loukopoulos, L. (2004) "The Limits of Expertise: The Misunderstood Role of Pilot Error in Airline Accidents." NASA Ames Flight Cognition lab - hot topic article

Dunning, D. and Kruger, J. (1999) "Unskilled and Unaware of It: How Difficulties in Recognizing One's Own Incompetence Lead to Inflated Self-Assessments," *Journal of Personality and Social Psychology*. DOI:10.1037/0022-3514.77.6.1121

Effectiviology. "The Benjamin Franklin Effect: How to Build Rapport by Asking for Favors." *Effectiviology*. www.effectiviolog.com

Effectiviology. "The Curse of Knowledge: A Difficulty in Understanding Less-Informed Perspectives." Effectiviology. *www.Effectiviology.com*

Effectiviology. "The Egocentric Bias: Why It's Hard to See Things from a Different Perspective." *Effectiviology. www.effectiviolog.com*

Effectiviology, "The Fundamental Attribution Error: When People Underestimate Situational Factors." *Effectiviology*. www.effectiviolog.com

Effectiviology. "The Ostrich Effect: Why and How People Avoid Information." *Effectiviology. www.Effectiviolog.com*

Ellison, K. (2015) "Being Honest About the Pygmalion Effect."*Discover.* www.Discover-Magazine.com

Elton; Gruber; Blake (1996). "Survivorship Bias and Mutual Fund Performance". *Review of Financial Studies.* **9** (4): 1097–1120. doi:10.1093/rfs/9.4.1097. S2CID 154097782

Farnam Street Blog. "Reciprocation Bias. *fs.* www.fs.blog

Farnam Street Blog. "Survivorship Bias: The Tale of Forgotten Failures." www.fs.blog

Fehr and Gächter.. (2000) "Fairness and Retaliation: The Economics of Reciprocity.". *Journal of Economic Perspectives.* 14 (3): 159–182. doi:10.1257/jep.14.3.159.

Festinger, L. and Carlsmith, J, (1957) "Cognitive consequences of forced compliance." .*Journal of Abnormal and Social Psychology.*www.-booksc.org/journal/12024

Festinger, L,. Riecken, H.,and Schachter, S. . (2019) *When Prophecy Fails Kindle Edition. www.kindlee-books@ AmazonSmile.*

Franchina, V., Vanden Abeele, M. van Rooij, A., *et al.* (2018) *International Journal of Public Health.* doi: 10.3390/ijerph15102319

Franklin, B. The Autobiography of Benjamin Franklin.

Fredrickson, B.; Kahneman, D. (1993). "Duration neglect in retrospective evaluations of affective episodes". *Journal of Personality and Social Psychology.*

65 (1): 45–55. doi:10.1037/0022-3514.65.1.45. PMID 8355141.

Gavrilova, A. "CO2 Out Of Sight, Not Out Of Mind." *The Decision Lab.* www.TheDecisionLab.com

Gilovich, T., Savistsky, K., and Medvee, V. (2000) "The Spotlight Effect in Social Judgment: An Egocentric Bias in Estimates of the Salience of One's Own Actions and Appearance." *Journal of Personality and Social Psychology,* 78(2), 211–222.

Harvey, F. (2019). "US is hotbed of climate change denial, major global survey finds." *The Guardian.* www.theguardian.com

Heath, C. and Heath D. (2006) "The Curse of Knowledge." *Harvard Business Revidew.* www.hbr.org

Hemprich-Bennett, D., Rabaiotti, D. and Kennedy, E. (2021) "Beware survivorship bias in advice on science careers. For objective careers advice, talk to those who left science as well as those who stayed." *Nature.* www.nature.com

Hendricks. K. (2016) "The decoy effect: Why you make irrational choices every day (without even knowing it)." *Kent Hendricks.* www.kenthendricks.com

Improbable Research.(2021) "Preview: 'The incompetence Opera.'" *Improbable Research: Research that Makes People Laugh and then Think. www.improbable.com*

The Investopedia Team. (2020) *Bandwagon Effect. Investopedia. www.investopedia.com*

iMoney Editorial.(2016) "Don't Fall Into The Gambler's Fallacy In Your Investment." iMoney Learning Center.www. iMoney.com

Investopedia Team. "Survivorship Bias Risk." Investing Essentials..www.investopedia.com/

Kahneman, D.; Ritov, I.; Schkade, D. (1999). "Economic Preferences or Attitude Expressions?: An Analysis of Dollar Responses to Public Issues" (PDF). *Journal of Risk and Uncertainty.* 19: 203–235. doi:10.1007/978-94-017-1406-8_8. ISBN 978-90-481-5776-1

Kahneman, D. (2011) *Thinking, Fast and Slow.*Kindle Edition. Doubleday, Canada.

Karawynn. (2012) "Salary negotiation: we've been doing it wrong." pocketmint: small change toward a rich life. www.ocketmint.net

King Universities Online. "The Psychology of FOMO." *King Universities Online. Ww.online.king.edu*

Kern, G. (2019) "Overcoming Anchoring Bias in Negotiations" *Risksavers; Managing the Human Side of Risk. www.risksavers.com*

KnowledgeOne. "3 cognitive biases to know in education." KnowledgeOne.3 cognitive biases to know in education - KnowledgeOne

Lazarus, R.J. (2009) "Super Wicked Problems and Climate Change: Restraining the Present to Liberate the Future." *Cornell Law Review.* Vol 84, Art. 8. www.-cornell.edu

Leaksy, R. and Lewin, R. (1992) *Origins Reconsidered: In Search of What Makes Us Human.* Anchor Books, a Division of Random House, Inc. New York

Lesage, D. (2019. "Heuristics vs. Biases: The Difference." Behavioral Economics; Cognitive Science; The Website.|www.medium.com

Martin, D.(2021) "Defend your business from plan continuation bias." elabor8. www.elabor8.com

McCloud, S. (2018) "Cognitive Dissonance." *Simply-Psychology. www.simplypsychology.org/*

McDermott, R. (1998) *Risk-Taking in International Politics: Prospect Theory in American Foreign Policy.* The University of Michigan Press, Ann Arbor, MI.

McRaney, D. (2011) "The Benjamin Franklin Effect." *You Are Not So Smart.* www.youarenotsosmart.com

Miller, B. (2018) "How the Halo Effect Impacts Your Workplace." *HR Daily Advisor. www.HRDailyAdvisor.blr.com,*

Miller, J. G. (1984)." Culture and the development of everyday social explanation." . *Journal of Personality and Social Psychology.* 46 (5): 961–978. doi:10.1037/0022-3514.46.5.961. PMID 6737211.

Murphy, M. (2017) "The Dunning-Kruger Effect Shows Why Some People Think They're Great Even When Their Work Is Terrible" *Forbes. www.forbes.com*

Nickerson, R. D., (1998) "Confirmation Bias: A Ubiquitous Phenomenon in Many Guises." *Review of General Psychology..*University of California San Diego. www.ucsd.edu

Norton, M, Mochen, D. and Ariely, D..(2012) "The IKEA effect: When labor leads to love." *Journal of Consumer Psychology* 22, 453-460.

O'Connor, A. M., (1989) "Effects of framing and level of probability on patients' preferences for cancer chemotherapy." *Journal of Clinical Epidemiology*,42(2), 119-126. doi:10.1016/0895-4356(89)90085-1

Ord, Toby (2020). *The Precipice: Existential Risk and the Future of Humanity.* United Kingdom: Bloomsbury Publishing. p. 67. ISBN 1526600218.

Pelly, S. (2021) 60 Minutes. Watch 60 Minutes Season 54 Episode 3: 10/3/2021: The Facebook Whistleblower, Unforgiven, The Final Act - Full show on CBS

Perera, A., (2021) "Framing Effect." *Simply Psychology.* www.SimplyPsychology.org

Phase. "The Curse of Knowledge Bias and How it Impacts Your Work." *Phase. www.Phase.com*

Pioneer Press. (2007) "The Baader-Meinhof Phenomenon? Or: The Joy Of Juxtaposition? (Responsorial) 23, 23, 23, 23, 23, 23, 23, 23, 23, 23, 23, 23, 23, 23, 23, 23, 23, 23, 23, 23, 23, 23!"Twin Cities Pioneer Press.www.twincities.com

Poundstone, W. (2016) "'I Wore the Juice'- The Dunning-Kruger Effect." Little, Brown and Company. www.medium.com

Psychology. "Law of Small Numbers." Psychology. *www.ResearchNet.com*

Radtke, T., Liszewska, N., Horodyska, K., Boberska, M., Schenkel, K., and Luszczynska, A. (2019). "Cooking together: The IKEA effect on family vegetable intake." *British Journal of Health Psychology*, 24(4), 896-912. https://doi.org/10.1111/bjhp.12385

Rath. S. and Georgieva. T. (2014) "No Startup Hipsters: Build Scalable Technology Companies." Creative Commons. ISBN-10 : 0996010602. ISBN-13 : 978-0996010603

Robinson, R. J., Keltner, D., Ward, A., and Ross, L. (1995) "Actual versus assumed differences in construal: 'Naive realism' in intergroup perception and conflict." *Journal of Personality and Social Psychology*, 68(3), 404-417. doi:10.1037/0022-3514.68.3.404

Rosenthal, R,. and Jacobson, L. (1968) *Pygmalion in the Classroom: Teacher Expectation and Pupils' Intellectual Development.* Holt, Rinehart and Winston, Inc. New York, NY.

Ross, L. and Ward, A. (1995). Psychological barriers to dispute resolution. In M. P. Zanna (Ed.), Advances in experimental social psychology (Vol. 27, pp. 255-304). San Diego, CA: Academic Press.

Ruhl, C. (2021) "Self-Serving Bias: Definition and Examples." *Simply Psychology. www.simplypsychology.org*

Sacred Texts. (2015) "The Code of Hammurabi: Hammurabi's Code of Laws: Paragraphs 100-199". www.sacred-texts.com.

Simon, H. A. (1992) "What Is an Explanation of Behavior?" *Psychological Science* 3.

Scott, E. (2021) "How to Deal With FOMO in Your Life: The Origin of FOMO and How It Affects Our Health." Verywellmind. www.verywellmind.com

Segal, D. (2021) medically reviewed by Ratini, M. "What is Confirmation Bias?" *WebMD. www.webmd.com*

Shepherd S. and Campbell T. (2020) "The Effect of Egocentric Taste Judgments on Stereotyping of Welfare Recipients and Attitudes Toward Welfare Policy" *Journal of Public Policy & Marketing.* https://doi.org/10.1177/0743915618820925

Shepherd, S., & Kay, A. C. (2012) "On the perpetuation of ignorance: System dependence, system justification, and the motivated avoidance of sociopolitical information." *Journal of personality and social psychology*, 102(2), 264.

Shonk, K.(2021) "What is Anchoring in Negotiation? Learn how to defuse the anchoring bias and make smart first offers." Harvard Law School Program on Negotiation." www.pon.harvard.edu,

Silfwer, J. "The Baader Meinho Penomomenon:Chances are that you will hear about this effect again, soon." www.doctorspin.org

Strough, J., Mehta, C. M., McFall, J. P., & Schuller, K. L., (2008) "Are older adults less subject to the sunk-cost fallacy than younger adults?" *Psychological Science, 19*(7), 650-652. Sunstein, C. "The Availability Heuristic, Intuitive Cost-Benefit Analysis, and Climate Change." The University of Chicago. s10584-006-9073-y.pdf (zlibcdn.com)

https://doi.org/10.1111/j.1467-9280.2008.02138.x

Thaler, R. (1980) "Toward a positive theory of consumer choice." *Journal of Economic Behavior & Organization, 1*(1), 39-60. https://doi.org/10.1016/0167-2681(80)90051-7

Thomas, L. (1979). The Medusa and the snail: More notes of a biology watcher. New York: Viking Press.

Tierney, J., (2011) "Do You Suffer From Decision Fatigue?" *The New York Times. ww.nytimes.com*

Tversky, A. and Kahneman, D. (1981) "Belief in the Law of Small Numbers." Hebrew University of Jerusalem. Psychological Bulletin 1971, Vol. 76, No. 2, 105-11. www.stats.org.uk

Tversky, Amos; Kahneman, Daniel (October 1983). "Extension versus intuitive reasoning: The conjunction fallacy in probability judgment". *Psychological Review.* 90 (4): 293–315. doi:10.1037/0033-295X.90.4.293. Archived from the originalon 2013-02-23.

Tversky, A. and Kahneman, D. (1981) "The Framing of Decisions and the Psychology of Choice." *Science.* www.(science.org

Van Cleeve, M. "The Small Numbers Fallacy." www.libretext.org

Viscusi, W. K, Magat, W A.,.and Hubert, J. (1987.) "An investigation of the rationality of consumer valuations of multiple health risks." *The RAND journal of economics,* 465-479.

Wai, J. and Rindermann, H. (2017)"What goes into high educational and occupational achievement? Education, brains, hard work, networks, and other factors." *High Ability Studies.* https://doi.org/10.1080/13598139.2017.1302874.

Wargo, E. (2006) "How Many Seconds to a First Impression?" APS: Association of Psychological Science. www.psychologicalscience.org

Webb, T. L., Chang, B. P., & Benn, Y. (2013). "'The ostrich problem': Motivated avoidance or rejection of information about goal progress." *Social and Personality Psychology Compass,* 7(11), 794-807. https://doi.org/10.1111/spc3.12071

Weyland, K, (2002). The Politics of Market Reform in Fragile Democracies: Argentina, Brazil, Peru, and Venezuela. Princeton, NJ: Princeton University Press.

Wikipedia, "Code of Hammurabi." Wikipedia. www.wikipedia.com

Williams, B. S. (2020 "Heuristics and Biases in Military Decision Making." Mission Command: Military Review. www.army.mil

WISEducation. "'When sticking to the plan makes us stuck': Plan continuation bias and university/career plans." WISEducation.www.wiseducationblog.com

Wolniewicz CA, Tiamiyu MF, Weeks JW, Elhai JD. Problematic smartphone use and relations with negative affect, fear of missing out, and fear of negative and positive evaluation. Psychiatry Res. 2018;262:618-623. doi:10.1016/j.psychres.2017.09.058.

Woods, H. C. and Scott, H. (2016)" #Sleepyteens: social media use in adolescence is associated with poor sleep quality, anxiety, depression and low self-esteem." *Journal of Adolescence*, 51, pp. 41-49. (doi:10.1016/j.adolescence.2016.05.008)

Wu, Bozhi. (2019) "Decision-Making Heuristics and Evolution." Bozhi's Website. www.wixsite.com

Zwicky, A. M. (2006) "Why are we so deluded?" Stanford University. Microsoft Word - LSA07.ab-st.doc (stanford.edu)

www.ingramcontent.com/pod-product-compliance
Lightning Source LLC
Chambersburg PA
CBHW051310130726
47987CB00004B/1735